FAITH
ELUCIDATIONS

ON HUMANITY, EVIL, CHRIST, THE SPIRIT, AND THE CHURCH

FAITH ELUCIDATIONS

ON HUMANITY, EVIL, CHRIST, THE SPIRIT, AND THE CHURCH

Rev. Dr. Emmanuel Clapsis

HOLY CROSS
ORTHODOX PRESS
Brookline, Massachusetts

Publication of this book was made possible, in part, through the generous contribution of Nickoletta and Demos Pirperis.
Cover design by Eleni Sophia Pirperis
Cover art by Dmitry Kalinovsky

Published by
Holy Cross Orthodox Press
Hellenic College, Inc.
50 Goddard Avenue
Brookline, MA 02445 USA

ISBN 9781960613110
      9781960613141 (epub)

Cataloging-in-Publication
(Provided by Cassidy Cataloguing Services, Inc.)
Names: Clapsis, Emmanuel, author.
Title: Faith elucidations : on humanity, evil, Christ, the Sprit, and the church
        / Rev. Dr. Emmanuel Clapsis.
Description: Brookline, Massachusetts : Holy Cross Orthodox Press, [2026]
            | Includes bibliographical references.
Identifiers: ISBN: 9781960613110 (Print) | 9781960613141 (epub)
Subjects: LCSH: Orthodox Eastern Church--Doctrines. | Theological
        anthropology. | Good and evil—Orthodox Eastern Church. |
        Jesus Christ--Person and offices. | Salvation--Orthodox Eastern
        Church. | Death--Orthodox Eastern Church. | Hell--Christianity.
        | Holy Spirit--Orthodox Eastern Church. | Spirituality--Orthodox
        Eastern Church.
Classification: LCC: BX320.3 .C53 2026 | DDC: 281.9--dc23

DEDICATION

To my beloved wife, Sapfo, whose unwavering love and support illuminate my path, and to our three wonderful children, George, Tony, and Theocharis, along with their families, whose love fill my heart with joy.

PROLOGUE

This volume is a collection of short theological articles reflects aspects of my theological and pastoral journey. They emanate from my theological studies, pastoral sensitivities, and moments of contemplation that often accompany one's quest for answers to life's profound questions. They advocate an engagement with the existential challenges Orthodox believers face as they struggle to live their faith meaningfully. Each article is a snapshot of my theological exploration and pastoral challenges at different stages, influenced by personal experiences, academic studies, and dialogical interactions with modernity's challenge to the Christian faith. I wrote these articles with the intention not only to articulate my thoughts on various theological issues but also to create a space for readers to wrestle with their Orthodox faith, encouraging them to think critically and reflectively about their self-understanding always through their active participation in the life of the Church. They promote a synthesis of faith and social responsibility, inspiring a future where faith, action, and community converge in powerful ways, enabling Orthodox believers to reflect the love of Christ in an increasingly fragmented world. Their life-sustaining and transformative relationships with God should become the basis of understanding their vocation to mediate God's presence in the world actively.

This collection reflects my conviction that theology is an evolving dialogue of the Christian Church that necessitates contributions from diverse perspectives and experiences. The collection encourages interdisciplinary dialogue, drawing on philosophy, history, and sociology to enrich the theological discourse. Theology must not exist in a vacuum but must actively engage with the cultural context in which it finds itself. As such, these articles connect the timeless truths of the faith with contemporary realities and challenges, making the discussion relevant for today's audience. In a world marked by rapid changes and complex challenges, the role of theology is more vital than ever. It is an anchor and a guide, inviting individuals to engage with Orthodox tradition and its implications of faith in their daily lives.

My objective is not merely to present a compilation of articles but to invite readers into a shared journey of discovery. Each piece is a conversation starter, a call to reflect on the nuances of belief and the complexities of living out one's faith in an ever-changing world. Through this collection, readers will find answers and be inspired to ask more profound questions, fostering their growth and nurturing a more profound understanding of the divine. These articles will serve as faithful companions to the reader's theological exploration, sparking curiosity and contemplation in a world that desperately needs thoughtful engagement with faith.

I

GOD'S LOVING
PRESENCE IN THE WORLD

The World discloses God's creating and life-giving love, which freely (ex nihilo) brought it into existence. The World is the subject of God's unconditional love.

But who is God, and how can we communicate our understanding of Who He is? Language – reflecting cultures, historical contexts, experiences, and beliefs – has limited potential to provide a comprehensive description or representation of Who God is. Referring to divine realities, St. John of Damascus expresses the antinomy that characterizes the tradition of the Orthodox Church on knowing and communicating the truth about God: "not all things are inexpressible, and not all are capable of expression, and neither are all things unknowable nor are they all knowable." As humans need to know and relate to God, we rely on images of Him based on the history of His Revelation. Such images of God, informed by the tradition of the Church, are not exact and fully represent who God is. It is idolatry to identify the multiple anthropomorphic images of God as accurate and comprehensive representations of God. Therefore, we must be cautious not to confuse what we think when we hear or speak the word "God" with God. Nevertheless, based on the history of His Revelation, it is possible to have a limited understanding of God. Such an understanding enables us to discern his salvific presence in the life of the World, our religious community, and our lives.

How, then, do we talk about God once we recognize that we cannot speak of God adequately but must say something? We do what the great users of language, poets, do when trying to tell the unsayable: we pile up metaphors and images. And so, we say that God is the creator, judge, parent, spouse, shepherd, king, lawgiver, rock, leader, Savior, and so on. But there must be some control over these metaphors. After all, some ways of describing God are abhorrent to the Christian tradition, e.g., God is evil or hatred. Is there a central metaphor for God that can provide a guideline for talking about God, a metaphor with which all other metaphors must be in accord to be deemed acceptable? The first fundamental metaphor for talking about God in Christianity is love (I Jn. 4.8,16). All other metaphors that we use for God must agree with it. Agape is love to which satisfaction is irrelevant. The lover seeks nothing from the beloved, not even gratitude. The lover gives the lover's self to the beloved. Thus, agape should be understood as a "self-gift," the gift of the self to the other asking nothing in response. Agape is a pure gift of self to the other.

In her proclamation and witness, the Church communicates this fundamental truth that God is a pure and perfect self-gift. It is important to remember that knowing God as agape, love does not describe God's name as a person, but rather, it signifies how He eternally exists in relation to His Word, the Holy Spirit, and His Creation. Thus, we know God, the creator of all that exists, in His relational mode. When we pray "in the name of the Father and of the Son and the Holy Spirit," we assert that God is to be thought of first not as "the one" but as the relatedness of "the three." Christians believe God is at the root of all that exists; He is an endless self-gift. When we use the word "God," the Mystery that grounds and surrounds all that exists, we speak of the infinite and eternal explosion of self-gift. If we are created in the image and likeness of God, and God is Triune, then ought we not be able to see traces of the Trinity in our experience?

Nothing exists if it is not loved. The World and humanity exist because God loves them. The created World gives nothing to God, but rather, God gives something to it, namely, Himself through Christ and the Holy Spirit. Why? Because God is like overflowing love. This overflowing love is the only reason for humanity's existence and the whole universe – everything that ever has, ever will, or ever can exist.

As human beings, our uniqueness in the complexity of the World is that we are capable of acknowledging that we are infinitely loved and either accepting or rejecting it. We can embrace being loved or deny it and turn away from it. Regardless of human beliefs and actions, God unconditionally loves all human beings and the World in a Godlike way. It is simply not the case that God loved you on Tuesday, but then on Wednesday you sinned, so God loved you less, but then on Thursday you repented, so God loves you again. Nothing that human beings can do can make God not love them. If there were, they would be more powerful than God in that they could cause God to change and cease to be unconditional love.

If God, in His love, sustains all creation and is present through the Holy Spirit that "fills all things," His presence may go unnoticed. What is everywhere present is more often than not unnoticed or taken for granted. What is always there gets little or no attention. So, there is a need for occasions that enable us to become aware in concrete terms of the presence of God. In the Orthodox tradition, we call such occasions mysteries/sacraments.

Mysteries/Sacraments, in a broader sense, refer to any person, place, thing, event, sight, sound, taste, touch, or smell that causes us to notice the love of God, which sustains and fills all that exists. How many such sacraments are there? The number is virtually infinite, as many as there are things in the universe. Nothing can become a sacrament for someone, absolutely nothing. This is reflected in the Eucharist, which encompasses and sanctifies the whole creation since all creation participates in God's sanctity and goodness. The reason for such inclusiveness is Orthodoxy's conviction that nothing is profane by definition. Everything is potentially sacramental. In the Liturgy, Creation and Humanity find their true nature in the unity with God; it reveals the destiny of the World because of God's benevolence. We are tasting God's love that sustains all that exists. The fact that God in Christ does not seem to be human or act humanly but has become human in every respect except sin implies that God participates in our humanity, and we, humans, participate through Christ in God's divine life. Thus, to be with God means to be fully human, filled by the presence of the Holy Spirit that enables us to live a life of love in Christ. Thus, whatever enhances and deepens our humanity makes us braver, wiser, more intelligent, more responsible, more accessible, more loving, and holy, i.e., like God.

II

BEING HUMAN

Advances in physical and human science and the experiences of living in a modern pluralistic society invite us to rethink what it means to be human. Orthodox theology can potentially contribute invaluable insights and fundamental perspectives on this question.

The Mystery of the Human Person

Orthodox theology insists that human beings cannot be fully understood by observing how they are or act as entities within the created world. God's relationship with the world and human beings' role in that relationship are defining elements of being. Against all kinds of reductionism, the Greek Fathers insisted that we cannot fully comprehend or explain what a human being is. Even the fact that human beings are created in the image of God does not define their humanity but signifies an intrinsic relation between God and human beings without determining what the image of God is.

As created icons of the uncreated God, humans are a mystery. They reflect the mystery of their archetype. As St. Gregory of Nyssa states: "An image is only genuinely such in so far as it expresses the attributes of its archetype." One of the characteristics of the Godhead is to be in its essence beyond our understanding, so the image should also express this. "Affirming the mysterious nature of humanity" is not an excuse to embrace anthropological agnosticism.

It suggests that humanity's nature must forever remain an open-ended question. Thus, the understanding of human beings is always subject to revision, correction, and enhancement through a process of conversation that includes the wealth of knowledge that people have accumulated through the centuries, the advances of sciences, and the experience of living in an ever-changing and increasingly pluralistic world.

How should theologians participate in such an open-ended conversation about the nature of humanity? Religion and science provide distinct but complementary insights about the world. St. Basil, in his sermons on the *hexaemeron*, makes clear that his language of faith has as its primary reason the salvation of people, which is not identical with the "persuasive language of human wisdom."[1] He leaves his listeners free to accept as plausible some rational explanations about the place of the earth in the universe. Still, he wants his listeners to transfer their admiration from nature to God, who has created order in the universe. Remembering the different orientations of theologians' and scientists' language helps us appreciate their contributions toward understanding the intricacies of being human. It sets the perimeters of the ongoing dialogue for the common good.

The Nature of Humanity

In the patristic tradition, a human being is often understood as a composite being consisting of body and soul. The soul is considered unique, indestructible, and sometimes immortal. At the same time, the body is understood as a dispensable part of a human being, a separate and inferior component of their nature. The patristic tradition has rigorously criticized the disjunction of body and soul. The human being is an embodied event. St. Gregory of Nazianzus stated that God, in the creation of man, united the spiritual and the material, the invisible and the visible elements of the created world. Being constituted by elements of the material and spiritual realities, St. Gregory considers man "a

---

1 Emmanuel Clapsis, "St. Basil's Cosmology," *Diakonia* 17(1982), pp. 62-74.

second cosmos, a great universe within a little one."[2] Each human being is an icon of the world. Since human beings reflect and hold together in their personhood the entire creation, they have the potential to reconcile the different levels of reality in which they participate and draw all into unity.

Humans are not created to dominate nature. It is their task to be like the world, diverse but united. As part of the natural world, humans must recognize and respect the diversity that characterizes the life of the material world as something that can be observed in their own lives. Human nature contains a fundamental and inseparable diversity of divine and human, earthly and heavenly, and material and spiritual elements. Because of these, human beings have as their vocation the uniting of the created world with its uncreated God. This mediational vocation of human personhood is realized in its fullest possible manner in Jesus Christ, in whom humanity and creation are forever united with God by the grace of the Holy Spirit. For this reason, Christ is the archetype of what it means to be human, the mirror in which one sees reflected one's true face and vocation.

Man as the Image of God

Human beings are not only *the* image of the world but also the image of God. Gregory of Nyssa locates the greatness of the human being "not in likeness to the created world, but in being in the image of the nature of the Creator."[3] Christian theologians, because of this relationship between God and humanity, will continuously borrow insights from their doctrine of God and their understanding of Jesus Christ to describe human dignity and vocation. What aspects of being human constitute the icon of God? Despite the extensive use of this concept in Scripture and the subsequent Christian tradition, we do not have a clear, exhaustive, and definitive description of what elements of human nature

---

2 *Orations* 38. 11 (PG 36. 321c-324b); Anna Stima Ellverson, *The Dual Nature of Man: A Study in the Theological Anthropology of Gregory of Nazianzus* (Uppsala/ Stockholm: Almqvist and Wiksell, 1981).

3 Greg. Nyssa. *Hom. Opif.* 16

reflect the image of God in every human being. It seems that this concept has assumed a variety of meanings that correspond to those aspects of human nature that theologians wished to extol for pastoral reasons: "Sometimes, for example, the expression 'in the image' refers to man's free will, or his rational faculty, or his characteristic of self-determination, sometimes to the soul along with the body, sometimes to the mind, sometimes to the distinction between nature and person, etc., and sometimes comprehensively to the whole man."[4] Thus, the concept of the "image" is a comprehensive term by which the Church expresses the distinctive *telos* of human life and it becomes the basis of moral exhortations.[5] The essential goodness of all human beings reflects their affinity with God, and this affinity is defined as the primary essential goodness of all human beings.

Human Personhood

What does it mean to be a person? For the philosopher John Locke, a person is an intelligent thinking being with reason and reflection. For the philosopher Immanuel Kant, rational beings are called persons because their very nature shows them to be ends in themselves. Finally, in the social philosophy of John MacMurray, persons are constituted by their mutual relation to one another. "I" exists only as one element in the complex "You" and "I." Generally, in Western philosophical thought, there is no significant distinction between person and individual; instead, the two terms are used almost interchangeably.

The Greek fathers, especially the Cappadocians, in their attempt to communicate the Christian faith in the triune God, developed a specific understanding of personhood that recognizes fundamental distinctions in the Godhead without endangering the oneness of God. By identifying the notion of hypostasis with the notion of person, they acknowledged that God is eternally Father, Son, and

---

4 Panayiotis Nellas, *Deification in Christ: The Nature of the Human Person* (New York: St. Vladimir's Press, 1987), p.22.
5 Jaroslav Pelikan, *Christianity, and Classical Culture* (New Haven & London: Yale University Press, 1993), p.125.

Holy Spirit, three distinct but relational *hypostaseis*. They spoke about a unique hypostatic identity and distinction 'within' God without postulating a difference in substance between the divine persons. Persons are unique and unrepeatable because their being is formed through and in relationships of love that allow difference to exist without fragmenting the unity of communion that love develops.

Orthodox theology grounded in the doctrine of the Trinity advocates that human beings cannot simply be reduced to self-referential entities. Human beings can never be separate, self-enclosed or self-sufficient entities. Their existence is verified in their relationships with one another, nature, and God. Thus, a person is not an individual but an open and ecstatic reality, referring to significant others for his or her existence. One becomes a person in self-transcendence, the movement of freedom toward communion.

The future of humanity depends on the quality of relationships that give existence to our being as persons. Only in relationships of love can we embrace the totality of the world and attain the fullness of our humanity. That fullness allows diversity and difference in a uniting world in which God loves, sustains, and desires us to partake of His glory.

III

BECOMING A PERSON

People, especially in times of social turmoil and uncertainty, interpret their personal or collective lives with all their accomplishments, failures, opportunities, and risks as the consequence of implicit or explicit anthropology. The perils that modernity has inflicted upon nature, the fragmentation of human consciousness, the despair and the violence that permeates modern society, and the crisis of primary communities of intimacy that gave until the dawn of modernity certainty and coherence to people's lives are not necessarily the consequences of moral failure or human negligence, but they are in a significant way the outcome of particular views about human beings that may need correction and even further development. New advances in physical and human science, a more sophisticated and reflective understanding of how human identities are formed, and the experience of living in a modern pluralistic society invite us to re-think what it means to be a human person. In response to such challenges, we are in a stage of searching for a new anthropology that emphasizes the interdependence of human persons with nature, provides a more significant space for tolerance of different ways of being a human being, and binds people into living communities of peace, justice, and love.

Living in a pluralistic modern society, we become increasingly aware that people of different races, religions, cultures, ethnicities, genders, and sexual preferences, despite their fundamental differences, can live and relate to each other in peace, sharing their human experiences and enriching their appreciation of life. Different theories and images of who and what a human person is may illuminate various aspects of human nature better than others. In a pluralistic society, people have opportunities to expand their horizons of understanding how people of different faiths, cultures, races, genders, and ethnicities can enrich each other's understanding and appreciation of humanity and conceive their irreducible differences as contributions of enrichment to the everyday life that we share and not as sources of division, conflict, and oppression. This presupposes that people are open to such a possibility once they have recognized the historicity and, therefore, provisionally of their plausibility structures that give meaning and coherence to their lives in the modern world. This openness makes us more tolerant of different views and modes of life and suspicious of ideologies that elevate anthropologies to universal truths. People, however, may reject the challenge of pluralism, ignore the advances of human and physical science, and insist that all must become, think, and act like them to be recognized by them as human persons.

What is the contribution of Greek patristic thought to this quest for a new anthropology? The Greek fathers have provided some invaluable insights and fundamental perspectives on what it means to be a human person that may illuminate our human condition in the modern world. Their understanding of being a person is not a fully blown, complete systematic theory of the nature of humanity. Their anthropological reflection is situated in the greater context of cosmology and the Christian beliefs about sin and redemption. They interpret the human condition from a theocentric perspective to facilitate the unity of the world with God. Their methodology reflects their conviction that the fullness of humanity can only be acquired as we unite ourselves with God. The sources of their reflections were the Gospel, the communal experience of faith, and the prevailing philosophical views of their times. Richard Norris is correct when he states that in the Christian tradition, theologians have tended, overall, to accept the commonplace wisdom of the culture in which it is set and then, in handling that wisdom, to revise and reshape it critically following the requirements of the language of Christian faith and hope.[1]

I hope that in this short presentation of such a profound and complex issue, I find the appropriate *public language* that helps others, who may or may not be theologians or Christians, learn something about human persons from the reflection of the Greek fathers or at least recognize some of the insights that the Greek fathers have advanced as elements of their understanding of human beings based on their different scholarly disciplines. The language of conversation is desirable and needs to be developed.

The Greek fathers believed humans could not be understood by observing how they function and relate. They suggested that God's relationship with the world and human beings' role in that relationship is a defining element of their view of humanity. Anthropology, for them, is derivative of their God-talk. Against all kinds of positivism, they insisted that we cannot fully understand or define what is a human person. Even the fact that human beings are created in the image of God does not define their humanity but signifies an intrinsic relation between God and human beings without determining what the image of God is in every human being. Human persons, as created icons of the uncreated God, are a mystery. They reflect the mystery of their archetype. Gregory of Nyssa stated: "... An image is only truly such in so far as it expresses the attributes of its archetype. One of the characteristics of Godhead is to be in its essence beyond our understanding, so the image should also express this."[2] Affirming the mysterious nature of humanity is not an excuse to embrace an anthropological agnosticism or to resign from any effort to understand as much as possible what it means to be a human person. It advocates an open anthropology suggesting that the fullness of humanity cannot be contained in any definition, expressed in, or described by any theory or constellations of theories about humanity. Thus, the understanding of human beings is always subject to revision, correction, and enhancement through a process of conversation that includes the wealth of knowledge that people

---

1   Richard Norris, 'Human Being," in Keeping the Faith, edit. G. Wainwright, p. 79
2   Gregory of Nyssa, On the Creation of Man, 11

have accumulated through the centuries, the advances of human and physical sciences, and the experience of living in an ever-changing and increasingly pluralistic world. How can theologians participate in such an open-ended conversation about human beings? St. Basil seems more liberal and open-minded than some twentieth-century Christians. In his homilies on the *hexaemeron,* he makes clear that his language of faith has as its primary reason the salvation of the people, and it is not identical with the "persuasive language of human wisdom." He leaves freedom for his listeners to accept as plausible some rational explanations about the place of the earth in the universe. Still, he wants his listeners to transfer their admiration from nature to God, who has ordered the universe. Remembering the different orientations that the languages of theologians and scientists use, it is always possible to appreciate each other's contribution and enrich our understanding of human personhood.

The Greek fathers believed that a human being is a composite being consisting of body and soul. They sharply distinguished body and soul and identified the human with the soul. The soul, for them, was unique, indestructible, and, for some fathers, immortal. At the same time, the body is a dispensable part of a human being, a separable and inferior component of their nature. Of course, such distinction reveals the platonic influence upon their thought, and the disjunction of body and soul has been rigorously criticized. The human person is an embodied event. St. Gregory of Nazianzus stated that God, in the creation of humans, united the spiritual and the material, the invisible and the visible elements of the created world: "Taking a body from the matter that He had previously created, and placing in it the breath of life that comes from himself, which Scripture terms the intelligent soul and the image of God, He (God) formed man as a second cosmos, a great universe within a little one."

The vocation of every human being is to keep these two aspects of our dual nature in harmony and even further to participate through God's grace in the life and glory of God. Each of us is an icon of the world. "You are a universe within the universe," states St. Nilus of Ancyra (early fifth century): "Look within yourself and see there the whole creation." Since every human person reflects and holds together in their person the entire creation, they have the potential to reconcile the different levels of reality in which we participate and draw them all into unity. That is why human beings were introduced last into the creation as a natural bond of unity. Human beings are not created to dominate nature since nature is their life. As part of the natural world, human beings must recognize and respect the diversity that characterizes the life of the material world as something that can be observed in their own lives. Human nature contains a fundamental and inseparable diversity of divine and human, earthly and heavenly, material and spiritual elements. Because of this, human persons have a vocation to unite the created world with its uncreated God. This mediational vocation of human personhood is realized in its fullest possible manner by Jesus Christ, the God-man. For this reason, Christ is the model of what it means to be human; the mirror I see reflects my true face and vocation. For the Greek fathers, Anthropology is an aspect of Christology.

Man as the Image of God

The ultimate stage in our mediatorial ministry is possible because the human person is not only a microcosm, the universe in miniature but also a *microtheos*, god in miniature. We are not simply *imago Mundi,* the image of the world, but also *imago Dei,* the image of God. Each is a created reflection of the uncreated Deity, a finite expression of God's infinite self-expression. St. Gregory of Nyssa locates the greatness of the human being "not in likeness to the created world, but in being in the image of the nature of the creator."[3] Human beings in the Christian tradition are created in the image of God. The concept of the "image" is a comprehensive term by which Christians express the distinctive telos of human life and becomes the basis of moral exhortation. For the Cappadocians, the imperative to perform morally good

---

3 Gre Nyss. *Hom. Opif.* 16

works was especially grounded in the universality of the image of God in the entire human race.[4] Despite the extensive use of this concept in Scripture and the subsequent Christian tradition, we do not have a clear, exhaustive, and definitive description of what elements of human nature reflect the image of God in human beings. It seems that this concept has assumed varied meanings that corresponded each time to what aspects of human nature theologians wished to extol for pastoral reasons: "Sometimes, for example, the expression "in the image" refers to man's free will, or his rational faculty, or his characteristic of self-determination, sometimes to the soul along with the body, sometimes to the mind, sometimes to the distinction between nature and person, etc., and sometimes comprehensively to the whole man."[5] Christian theologians will borrow insights from their doctrine of God and their understanding of Jesus Christ to describe God's active presence in human beings. Such a process presupposed that these divine elements could be imperfectly reflected in the human image of God. Whatever excellence and goodness could be observed in the life of human beings was attributed to the active presence of God's image in them.

Human Personhood

What makes an animated being a human person? Is it possible to be without being a person? What does it mean to be a person? Adrian Thatcher discerns six different uses of personhood in Western philosophical thought. In theology, it designates the "threeness" of God, the one God is said to consist of three Persons. In ontology, the person is defined by their identity or essential difference from non-persons. Locke claimed that a person was a thinking, intelligent being, with reasons and reflection, and can consider itself the same thing in different times and places. In psychology, the term 'personality' refers to the particular

---

4   Jaroslav Pelikan, *Christianity and Classical Culture* (New Haven & London: Yale University Press, 1993), p.125.
5   Panayiotis Nellas, *Deification in Christ: The Nature of the Human Person* (New York: St. Vladimir's Press, 1987), p.22.

character that an individual acquires. In moral philosophy, Kant observes that rational beings are called persons because their very nature shows them to be ends in themselves, something that cannot be used simply as a means. In existentialism, the person is what they make of him or herself. Finally, according to the social philosophy of John Macmurray, persons "are constituted by their mutual relation to one another." "I" exists only as one element in the complex "You" and "I". There is no significant distinction between person and individual in Western philosophical thought, but quite the contrary, the two terms are sometimes used interchangeably. The work of John MacMurray, Martin Buber, and other social philosophers is a much-desired liberation from an excessive bias toward individuality. Contemporary Greek theologians, most notably Metropolitan John Zizioulas and Christos Yannaras have extensively studied the contribution of Greek patristic tradition on personhood. They believe that the Greek fathers, especially the Cappadocians, in their attempt to express the Christian faith in the one God who is triune, Father, Son, and Holy Spirit, developed a specific understanding of personhood that allows them to affirm hypostatic distinctions in the Godhead without endangering his oneness. Their concern was understanding and speaking about God as Father, Son, and Spirit without cave-in to tritheism or modalism. According to Metropolitan John Zizioulas, they achieve this purpose by identifying two distinct and not interchangeable concepts, the concepts of hypostasis and person. Hypostasis was loosely used to describe how the *ousia* (substance) exists as a concrete entity, and ousia was referred to as hypostasis. The concept of person was associated in Greek theater with the *prosopon* (mask), by which humans tried to free themselves from the oppression of the rational necessity of a unified and harmonious world. In the Roman world, *persona* signified the role that someone plays in social and legal relationships. In both instances, the *prosopon* or *persona* had nothing to do with ontology. It is something added to a human being associated primarily with freedom and relationality. Referring to the Trinity as one God, three hypostases, or one God, three persons could be interpreted as accepting tritheism or embracing modalism. Their challenge was to give ontological content to each person of the Trinity without endangering biblical monotheism and God's absolute freedom. Their response to this challenge was to identify hypostasis with the person. As an event of freedom and relationality, a person gains ontological content through this identification. They could speak about a unique hypostatic identity and distinction 'within' God without postulating a difference in substance between the divine persons.

What is the anthropological significance of this development? More particularly, what can theologians contribute to the public discussion of what it means to be human? The person is no longer something added to a being, but it is itself the hypostasis of being; in other words, freedom and relationality are categories that express how personhood and being are formed and developed. This means that for our study of human beings, it is inadmissible to deal with the nature or substance of human beings by referring only to what they are in themselves. Human persons can never be separate, self-enclosed, and self-sufficient entities. Their existence is verified in the relationships that they have with others other than themselves, and that other includes the natural world.

Thus, a person is not an individual but an open and ecstatic reality referred to by others for their existence. The actualization of personhood occurs in self-transcendence, the movement of freedom toward communion with other persons. The other aspect of personhood identified with freedom affirms that persons become communion and affirm the existence of each other only as they freely relate through love to others than themselves. In such a relational context, people develop their unique and unrepeatable way of being without such differences threatening their communion with other beings.

IV

THE HUMAN PREDICAMENT

Modernity's excitement that the advances of human science and knowledge will free the world from injustice, violence, oppression, poverty, and human suffering has faded. In the present world, people and human communities are fragmented, polarized, mistrusting, and competing with one another, seeking to protect their particularity and interests through exclusionary attitudes. The insistence on human possibilities in an ideal virtual world was too optimistic.

In Christian tradition, the pervasive presence of evil in the world is recognized along with the belief about the good possibilities human beings have because the benevolence of God has gifted them. Thus, Christianity is neither simply optimistic nor pessimistic; it appreciates the goodness of the essential nature of every human being. At the same time, Christianity recognizes the evil human beings can commit against themselves, the world, and humanity. In personal and collective life, humans can experience the goodness of the material world and the evil that pervades it. Christ came to the world to liberate humanity from evil and unite the whole creation with God through God's Spirit. Our understanding of what God has achieved for humans and the world through Jesus Christ presupposes a knowledge of the nature of evil in the world from which humans seek redemption and God.

Evil is a universal, pervasive reality. We live in a world filled with crises, fear, and the shadow of "unresolvable threats." Seeking to understand the pervasiveness of the evil that prevails in the present world, we adopt attitudes and beliefs that frequently obscure its causes. We tend to blame the particular people, leaders, groups, or forces involved in these unwanted events, as if, were they only not the way they are now, the problem would recede or vanish. However, if everyone is saying and feeling this about everyone else – which seems to be the case in family conflicts, minor town squabbles, corporations or city governments, among classes, races, and nations – the theory that the problem is all the fault of one group is hardly credible. The cause cannot lie uniquely in this or that group when all share the same symptoms: the capitalists, the unions, the communists, the unenlightened and irrational public, the politicians, the priests, or the king. Instead, we all augment the evils that prevail in the world by our choices, attitudes, and actions.

Our culture leads us to believe that even if we all are the sources of evil in the world, the situation certainly will change – it will not always be so. In the past, corruption was more widespread than now and more brutal in its expression. Brutality, violence, injustice, and untold suffering are receding with time, the development of civilizations, and especially the growth of science, labor-saving inventions, education, and moral ideals. Whether the world is better now than in the past remains a moot point; in any case, relations are gentler, people more lawful, the government powerless and less harsh, laws more equal and just, and customs less demanding on the weak. This kind of improvement is regarded as a fixed law of history. However, we must recognize that the developed science and technology, the nearly universal education, and modern culture's progressive moral and social ideals have neither eradicated nor substantially lessened the human problem. Although unquestionably significant advances have been made in the world, violence, oppression, conflict, fatedness, lostness, and despair stalk our society's hearts, streets, and public life. Though many symptoms of evil have been drained off, so to speak, the pot of human evil seems to be bottomless. But where does this infinite brew come from? Why are we all this way; why is social life – not to mention family life – so full of conflicts, and why is history so brutal, lethal, and terrifying? Here, there have been significant disagreements.

It has been argued that people become insensitive, brutal, unjust, and violent because of damage to their psyche. A leading analyst has noted that if only peoples' neuroses could be straightened out, they could become authentic persons again, and our social problems would disappear. Thus, through therapy, people could again become rational and moral persons. On the other hand, existential philosophers have attributed evil to the inward self. They advocate that the problem lies in inner emptiness and outer conformity; the answer is personal decisions, self-affirmation, and self-direction. Those who embrace this interpretation of social evil believe in their open, individualist, fluid society and the democratic process created to resolve its continuing problems. They tend to regard society and its institutions as relatively healthy because they are malleable to that democratic process. Consequently, they have been apt to locate the source of the deeper problems of life in the inward psyche and the answers to these problems in education, therapy, and moral or religious conversion.

Another view advocates that society molds individuals and not the reverse. So, the deeper level of the problem lies in the objective social sphere, in the unjust and unequal forms of social institutions. From this perspective, the emphasis on the psyche appears not only naïve but self-serving. It is a typical bourgeois "cop-out," a theory that more illustrates the human problem than clarifies or resolves it. Furthermore, from this view, the problem lies in the character of the objective social order, not within the soul; only a radical political, economic, social, structural, or institutional change in that order will affect the resolution of the human problem. Each of these two views has a firm grasp on the one end of this polarity and ignores the other – with unfortunate intellectual and social results.

Others argue that unchecked human impulses are at fault for the evil in the world. They advocate that wherever impulse rules, a reappearance of primal chaos occurs. Where intelligence and a will submissive to intelligence govern, there is order and harmony, so humanity appears. The weakness of this argument is not its emphasis on rationalism and intelligence since both are qualities essential to all forms of human creativity and fulfillment. The liability of this argument lies in the assumption that intelligence and rationality can be "pure," free of shame, prejudice, bias, self-interest, and willpower, especially in situations of anxiety and threat. It is possible for them that fully developed intelligence can be universal, transcending and controlling the local interests of the self or its group. But, of course, a highly developed intelligence can be, in concrete life situations, an instrument of the specific self and its will to power. Since intelligence can, like an impulse, become the tool of the self, the problem lies more profound than the polarity represented by these two ancient antagonists.

Thus, the evil that permeates personal and social life is not just psychological maladjustments or faulty social institutions. Nor is there a lack of knowledge of hard, clear thinking or correct theory about humans and the world. Through all these interpretations of evil, the self, as a self-contained entity, seems to use impulses and intelligence to cause conflicts. Thus, the finite self is finite and is to be blamed. The self depends on all sorts of conditions and forces out of control, bound to groups, hemmed in by specific perspectives, and governed by partial aims. The self is a self in the world, and it is attachment to the self, others, and its world that constitutes the human problem. Finitude, creatureliness, and the love of both are at fault.

One of the problems of talking intelligibly and empirically about the human predicament has now been uncovered. On the one hand, this predicament appears in experience to be quite a universal state and a given like the human condition itself, almost as if we were tragically fated to it. Thus, some of the usual explanations we have discussed view evil as a given reality and human responsibility. On the other hand, we experience our involvement in human trouble as personal, individual, and free, as something for which we are responsible and blameworthy. Thus, the evil we commit is unnecessary, something inherent in our nature and determines us, but it is something we want and choose. Here arise the two types of language that one meets on this theme in sociology, psychology, philosophy, and theology: certainty, necessity, and universality, and the language of choice, will, and freedom. Any sociological, psychological, philosophical, or theological explanation that ignores or explains away either side – the fateful and tragic or the free and responsible side – will prove both unempirical and inconsistent.

For Christians, the human predicament is not something that has just "happened to us" from the outside. It is not part of the given, our dependence, our temporality, and our mortality. As is shown by the universal experience, everyone in natural relations with others knows and assumes that our predicament is something our freedom has done and does. If this is so, then this general condition of our existence, in some strange way, is like a particular action that we decided at some moment to do and then proceed to carry out. It is something for which we feel responsible and blameworthy – though we may deny both. Christian belief and experience refuse to accept the view that our human predicament is an aspect of our nature as finite beings. Being created in God's image implies that we are experiencing the goodness of our creaturely finitude as creative possibilities inherent in our nature and activated through freedom that defines the future of our being.

The essential affirmation of the inherent goodness of humanity is grounded upon the experience of God as a unifying ground of human existence. Thus, the frailty of our finitude does not determine us since God, through His benevolence, can transform us. Furthermore, being human demands the cognizance that as created beings, it is to know that, although universal, estrangement is warping the human situation and not its essence, that being finite is not necessarily estranged. Therefore, Christian anthropology's essential structure of our humanity, its self-transcending finitude, its dependence, and its relations to the world and others are potentially good because God created and upheld them.

V

ALIENATION FROM GOD

The world and humanity are ambivalent. While they reflect their divinely granted essential goodness, they are also subject to the destructive forces of destruction. Nature can negate life through natural evil. Suffering, violence, injustice, oppression, physical and psychological illness, or premature death are epiphenomena of human finiteness and mortality, of the fact that we are not yet what we are supposed to be according to God's intention. People, in their alienation from God, sin against one another and contribute to the augmentation of evil in the world.

Human beings, as finite, created beings, are always under the threat of returning to nothingness out of which they have been made (*ex nihilo*) despite their inherent desire to live and to overcome the limitation of death. They commit evil acts against one another in perceiving the other's as threatening their self-interests and well-being. The benign nature of humanity is expressed in their existential struggle to control their unconscious instincts through the moral principles and values of their religious faith. St. Paul vividly described this existential struggle:

> I do not understand my actions. I do not do what I want, but I do the very thing I hate. I agree that the law is good if I do what I do not wish to. But in fact, it is no longer I that do it, but sin that dwells within me. For I know that nothing good dwells within me, that is, in my flesh. I can will what is right, but I cannot do it. For I do not do the good I want, but the evil I do not want is what I do.

Now if I do what I do not want, it is no longer I that do it, but sin that dwells within me.

So, I find it to be a law that when I want to do what is good, evil lies close at hand. For I delight in the law of God in my inmost self, but I see in my members another law at war with the law of my mind, making me captive to the law of sin that dwells in my members. Wretched man that I am! Who will rescue me from this body of death? (Rom 7.15-24)

For St. Paul, instincts are hostile to human persons, and he identifies them with evil.

The anthropocentric secular culture of modernity views humanity primarily as a material, natural reality subject to natural forces and needs. It defines the nature of society without any reference to God. Human activities are expressions of natural necessities, the instinct of self-preservation, and the "principle" of pleasure. Thus, modernity attributes to nature particular given functions, but it does not raise questions of meaning (cause and purpose) and consequently excludes any consequent regulative (moral) principles from human life. But, when the reference to cause and purpose is abolished, any criterion of *good* and *evil* is also abolished. Nature is that which is neither good nor evil, and Man is a part or manifestation of Nature. In this naturalist perspective, *good* and *evil* are conventional concepts, products of social circumstances. They reflect subjective experiences of the individual's pleasure or displeasure, unstable and shifting events in one's life that remain unfathomable.

The Christian Interpretation of Evil and Sin

The Orthodox Church affirms the essential goodness of creation, an act of God who is goodness-in-itself and the source of all goodness. The integrity of creation is unequivocally and normatively expressed in Scripture: "God saw everything that he had made, and behold, it was perfect" (Gen 1.31). Thus, since God created the world and assessed it to be "very good" then "God is not the cause of evil. Evil is the consequence of humanity's alienation from God, affecting their relationship with God and how they choose to relate to one another and nature.

In Orthodox theological tradition, humanity's alienation from God is expressed through the notion of "ancestral sin." It signifies humanity's conscious failure to live harmoniously and lovingly with God and nature. Instead, they turned by exercising their freedom to themselves and disregarding the will of God. This is their sin; this is the cause of their fall. Human self-sufficiency is against human nature - it negates what a human being is, i.e., depending on God and destined to live in communion with God. Human life is realized not as an autonomous experience but as a dependence on God, nature, and others. St. Gregory of Palamas concludes, "Instead of joy in the presence of God, the man preferred a selfish joy of which he was the object."

Humanity alienated itself from God through the harmful use of its freedom. This alienation/sin is the root cause of all evil. The notion of sin that generates corruption refers to whatever separates human beings and creation from God and the outcome of this separation. Man's choice to live apart and independently of God indicates his failure to realize his distinctiveness and freedom by falling away from the fullness of existence, which is the life of the Trinity, personal co-inherence, and communion in love. This falling away is sin, the failure of persons to realize their existential "end" to confirm and conserve the uniqueness of their existence through life. According to St. Maximus the Confessor, sin is a reality contrary to nature since it fragments and destroys nature; it is separation from being and exclusion from life.

Despite their alienation from God, humans continue to be an icon/image of God since their refusal to be with God or to oppose His will and ignore His love does not mean they cease to be His creation. God's image in sinful humanity is obscured and darkened but never lost. Yet, man alienating themselves from God brings themselves death and return to nothingness since they, as created and finite beings, cannot transcend the limitations of their created nature. Thus, death surfaces in the refusal of humanity to move beyond its created and finite nature and live with God. The epiphenomenon of this refusal is the evil humans generate through the harmful use of their freedom.

In God's original plan, humanity was intended to move freely towards unity with Him, participating in God's glory. But instead of doing this, humans have produced disharmony and discord within themselves and between the world and God. Christ, the very presence of God in history, liberates humanity and creation from evil and death. He is the One who brings all Creation in unity with God. In His person, all created things are "summed up" and "recapitulated" (Eph. 1.10); He draws them all together, holds them all in unity (Col. 1.17), and offers them all back to the Father. For the Church, Christ is the priest of creation, the model of man's proper relation to God and the natural world. Christ is not only the physical presence of God in the world but also the archetype of what it means to be human. In other words, we become truly human as we identify our existence with Christ and live His life pattern.

VI

THE DEVIL AND HIS LIMITATIONS

Scripture states that "The Son of God appeared for the very purpose of undoing the Devil's work" (John 3.8). Christ's death broke the power of the Devil (Heb. 2.14). Why did God become man to undo the Devil's work and liberate humanity and creation from death, the power of the Devil?

In the Christian tradition, the Devil(s) refers to "fallen angels," also known as demons. The article (ὁ) denotes Lucifer, the chief of the demons, as in Matthew 25.41, "the Devil and his angels." In Scripture, we have sparse allusions that speak of the Devil as the fallen angels (Rev. 12.7-9, Jude 1.6; cf. 2 Pet 2.4; Isaiah 14.12-15ff; Job 4.18). Jesus seems to subscribe to this belief. "I saw Satan like lightning falling from heaven" (Lk. 10.18). Scriptural references to the fallen angels and their identification with the Devil provided an interpretation of how evil emerged in God's good creation.

St. John of Damascus summarizes the biblical and patristic tradition about the Devil as a fallen angel.

> One of these angelic powers was chief of the terrestrial order and had been entrusted by God with the custody of the earth. Although he was not evil by nature, and although he had been made for good and had in himself not the slightest trace of evil from the Creator, he did not keep the brightness and the dignity that the Creator had bestowed upon him. By his free choice, he turned from what was according to nature to what was against it. Having become stirred up against the God who created him and

having willed to rebel against Him, he was the first to abandon sound and become evil. Evil is no more than the privation of good, just as darkness is the absence of light.[1]

The Devil possesses wickedness by free choice, not through a natural opposition to the good.[2] The Devil's sin is not innate but a reflection of their free choice to oppose God's will. Thus, evil originates not in God but in the Devil's will. "For nothing vile comes from the beautiful, nor does evil come from virtue."[3]

Why does the Devil work against the unity of humankind with God? St. Basil gives the following explanation:

> Because, being a receptacle of all evils, he also accepted the disease of malice and envied our honor. For he could not bear our life free from pain in paradise. With tricks and contrivances, he thoroughly deceived the human being, and, misusing his desire for likeness to God to deceive him, he showed him the tree and promised that he would be made like God through eating it. "For if you eat," he said, "you will be like gods, knowing good and evil" [Gen 3.5]. Accordingly, he was not fashioned as our enemy, but out of jealousy, he stood against us in enmity. Seeing himself thrown down from among the angels, he could not bear to see the earthly one lifted through progress to the rank of the angels.[4]

The opposition of Satan against God's "good creation" is unceasingly active. The Devil's operation in the world can be seen in the lives of people who have been subjected to his vile, either temporarily or permanently, and oppose God's divine will and love. All cultural elements, practices, and morals that contradict the Christian gospel have their origins and inspiration from the Devil and his demons. Even the heresies and schisms that besieged the life of the Church are attributed to the Devil.

In the patristic tradition, humans who have turned to

---

1 *De Fide Orthodoxa*, 2 :3, PG 94, p. 876
2 St. Basil, *On the Human Condition*, trans Nonna Verna Harrison (Crestwood, N.Y.: St. Vladimir's Seminary Press, 2005), p. 76
3 Basil the Great, *God is Not the Author of Evil* 8, PG 31.341. B-C.
4 Ibid.

themselves, separated from God, and opposed His will and love are believed to be under the Devil's influence. The ancestral sin of Adam and Eve is attributed to his instigation: "By the envy of the Devil, death came into the world" (Wisdom 2.24). For St. Basil, "Evil consists in estrangement from God. With a small eye turning, we *face the sun or our body's shadow. Thus,* one who looks upward easily finds illumination, but darkening is inevitable for one who turns toward the shadow." While St. Basil attributes the origins of evil to the Devil, he also considers that evil is committed by people who have been estranged from God and subject to their self-desires. In any case, the Devil as a fallen angel is a celestial being that we as humans discern from his operation in people who commit evil acts. Graphic images of the Devil have evolved throughout history based on human perceptions of the wicked people have experienced and the horror of his devious operation. By the end of the Middle Ages, the Devil had become horned, trident-wielding with hooves for feet and a long tail that has endured to modern times. While such an image portrays people's abhorrence of the Devil, his operations are certainly much more seductive than these images depict.

The Devil's sovereignty is constrained by the freedom God has bestowed on every human being. In the words of St. John of Damascus, the Devil has no power or strength against anyone unless he is invited or permitted to act in and through them. Therefore, while the Devil and his cohorts have conceived all evil and impure passions and have been allowed to visit attacks upon man, they cannot force anyone, for it is in our power either to accept the visitation or not.

Why does God allow the Devil to tempt humans and lead them to perdition? Why aren't human beings sinless in their nature so that the will to sin and so much suffering would not exist? St. Basil responds:

> God does not love what is constrained but what is accomplished out of virtue. And virtue comes into being out of free choice and not out of constraint. But free choice depends on what is up to us. And what is up to us is self-determined. Accordingly, the one who finds fault with the Creator for not fashioning us *by* nature sinless is no different from one who prefers the no rational nature

to the sensible, and what lacks motion and impulse to what has free choice and activity.[5]

The Devil does not have the power to foretell or determine the future of human beings. St. John of Damascus categorically states:

> Neither the angels of God nor the evil spirits know the future. Nevertheless, they foretell it. The angels do so when God reveals the future to them and orders them to foretell it, for whatever they say happens. On the other hand, the evil spirits foretell the future, sometimes by seeing the things that happen far ahead and sometimes by guessing them. For this reason, one must not believe them, even though they may often speak the truth in the manner we have spoken.[6]

Thus, in Orthodoxy, the Devil is considered the first cause of sin, which takes humans away from their journey towards unity. Man is a victim of the Devil's deception and co-responsible for sin. The Devil, however, does not have the power to destroy God's good creation. If that were the case, the Devil would have defeated God's benevolence and His plans for the future of His beloved creation

---

5 St. Basil, *On the Human Condition*, Trans. Nonna Verna Harrison (Crestwood, N.Y.: St. Vladimir's Seminary Press, 2005), p. 75
6 *De Fide Orthodoxa*, 2:3, PG 94, p. 877.

VII

HELL:

SEPARATION FROM GOD

Although the doctrine of hell is one of the cornerstones of traditional Christian belief, it currently lacks popularity among believers. Rarely does one hear this doctrine explicitly addressed in a Christian church today. Indeed, it would not be an exaggeration to assert that the average Christian believer struggles to explain what role (if any) the doctrine of hell plays in their faith.

Given these circumstances, it is crucial to revisit the origins of hell and investigate its development within the broader context of the Christian tradition. We will explore the evolution of hell in the Old Testament, during the Second Temple period (approximately 536-70 AD), in the New Testament, and various non-canonical Christian literature. We aim to identify the fundamental elements of this belief that have influenced the development of hell and its role in the church's kerygma and the lives of its community members. Is there a singular definition of hell within the biblical tradition?

The biblical texts regarding hell provide limited and fragmented information about the world of the dead and, by extension, the nature of hell. The language in these biblical references is rich in imagery and metaphors. Some images, such as fire and hell, which will be discussed later, take on a stereotypical character and later appear in the New Testament as synonyms for the eternal punishment awaiting the wicked. Parables and symbolic language are understandable, considering these descriptions reflect realities beyond human knowledge. However, this raises two questions: first, how should these representations be interpreted, and second, is it legitimate to understand such images literally and establish literal descriptions as the basis for systematic teaching about hell and the posthumous fate of individuals? If they are merely adaptations of a transcendent reality to the language and dimensions of human understanding, the safest approach to interpretation is similar to that used today for parables and metaphors. In this case, in contrast to allegory, there is no one-to-one correspondence of all elements of the image with spiritual reality; rather, the focus is on a central point that embodies the core meaning of the image.

The above observation is closely linked to the diversity evident in the representations and terminology used in biblical references regarding the human state after death. Beyond a looseness in description, this diversity primarily signifies the presence of various traditions and perceptions surrounding the afterlife and an evolution in the understanding of this concept. The coexistence of these different traditions and perceptions indicates an ongoing evolution in how it is understood. Furthermore, the existence of various images in specific texts – especially in the New Testament – suggests that this evolution does not negate the earlier stages of tradition; instead, they continue to exist independently or alongside the new elements that emerge. Moreover, God's revelation is given to us in the totality of Scripture, encompassing not only the synopsis but also the Old Testament, the writings of St. Paul, the Gospel of St. John, and the Book of Revelation. This implies that our understanding of hell should reflect the entirety of Scripture, maintaining a tense relationship between the different conceptions of hell that we find within them.

Furthermore, we interpret the Scriptures, especially concerning the complexity and diversity of perspectives presented by the teachings of the holy Fathers. They are the infallible teachers of the Church and the bearers of unadulterated Tradition; therefore, Holy Scripture cannot be understood outside their God-inspired teachings. After all, the Church – the divine-human Body of Christ – writes and interprets Holy Scripture. The consensus among the holy Fathers of the Church is that heaven and hell exist not from God's perspective but from humanity. Certainly, heaven and hell represent two ways of life, but it is not God who created them.

Afterlife in the Hebrew Bible

Hell, as a realm of eternal suffering and punishment, does not exist in the Old Testament. The early Israelites viewed death as the end of life for all people. When individuals die, their flesh returns to the dust from which it was formed (χους Gen 2.7; Ps 103.14). Their soul (ψυχή), sometimes referred to as the spirit (πνεῦμα), endures beyond the demise of the flesh and departs to *Sheol*, an underground dusty and gloomy place, a vast prison with gates and guard from which no one can escape. *Sheol* is also known as "the pit" (λάκκος), 'grave' synonymous with 'death' (θάνατος), and with the 'grave' or place of the dead. However, in Hebrew and Greek thought, Sheol/Hades was not a place of punishment for the wicked; it was where the souls of *all* the dead go. Here, all hope is gone (Ps. 143.3; cf. Wis. 13.100), and God has no more dealings with the departed, who are forgotten forever (Ps. 88.10ff; Eccl.2.16).

In *Sheol*, souls exist as shades, or *Rephaim*, in a dark world. Although they possess some form of "existence" and may even be conscious enough to speak, they are undeniably considered the dead (Ps. 7.6; Pss. 48.14; 54.15; 88.48; 116.3; Job 33.22; Hos. 13.14). Therefore, the common term for the ψυχή in *Sheol* is νεκρός.

Second Temple Judaism: Resurrection and the Myths of Israel

The rising influence of Hellenism within Second Temple Judaism, particularly the conflict under Antiochus Epiphanes and the ensuing struggles of the Maccabees, fomented a conceptual change. This change posited that the souls of faithful Jews would be rewarded and led to a place of blessing, in stark contrast to the souls of the wicked, apostate Jews, which would be directed to a place of eternal punishment. God, in His righteousness and goodness, could not treat the virtuous and faithful Jews the same way as the wicked.

While it was previously assumed that upon death, the soul or spirit of all persons is released from the body to Hades, a distinction began to emerge regarding the souls of the righteous and the wicked. One of the earliest and most explicit expressions of this change, which distinguishes the fate of the righteous from that of the evil, is found in Daniel 12.1-3:

> At that time Michael, the great prince, the protector of your people, shall arise [ἀναστήσεται] … at that time your people shall be delivered [ὑψόω], everyone who is found written in the book. *Many of those who sleep in the dust of the earth shall awake [ἐξεγείρω], some to everlasting life, and some to shame and everlasting contempt.* Those who are wise shall shine like the brightness of the sky, and those who lead many to righteousness, like the stars forever and ever.

In apocryphal and pseudepigraphical literature, the souls of the righteous head in a different direction than those of the wicked. The book of Sirach notes, 'It is easy for the Lord on the day of death to reward individuals according to their conduct' (Sir. 11.26). First Enoch 1–36 (second century BCE) is perhaps the earliest text in Judaism to express explicit divisions within Sheol for the righteous and the wicked. The author asserts, 'You, souls of the righteous … Be not sad that your souls have gone down into *Sheol* in sorrow, for there is the promise of restoration' (1 En. 102.4f.). This is further emphasized in the Wisdom of Solomon (first century BCE): 'The souls of the righteous are in the hand of God . . . they are at peace … their hope is full of immortality … they will govern nations and rule over peoples … the Lord will reign over them forever … they will stand with confidence [and] will receive a glorious crown' (Wis. 3.1, 7; 5.1, 15). For the wicked, however, their spirits wander about in torment (4 Ezra 7.80-99). For them, 'there will be no resurrection to life!' (2 Macc. 7.14).

Thus, the significant change within Second Temple Judaism lies in the distinction between righteous and wicked souls after death and their final place of residence. The virtuous soul ascends to a place of blessing, while the wicked soul descends to a place of torment.

Afterlife in Paul

In the earliest writings of the New Testament, particularly the authentic letters of the apostle Paul, there is no mention of Hades, *Gehenna*, the 'pit,' or 'hell.' In passage that is the oldest references of the New Testament to the *eschaton* (1 Thessalonians 4.13-18), St. Paul describes the *parousia*, the coming of the Lord,

> But we do not want you to be uninformed, brothers, about those who are asleep, that you may not grieve as others do who have no hope. For since we believe that Jesus died and rose again, even so, through Jesus, God will bring with him those who have fallen asleep. For this we declare to you by a word from the Lord, that we who are alive, who are left until the coming of the Lord, will not precede those who have fallen asleep. For the Lord himself will descend from heaven with a cry of command, with the voice of an archangel, and with the sound of the trumpet of God. And the dead in Christ will rise first. Then we who are alive, who are left, will be caught up together with them in the clouds to meet the Lord in the air, and so we will always be with the Lord. Therefore encourage one another with these words.

In the *parousia* both the dead and the living will meet the Lord. They will follow him to the heavens, where they will be with Him. In this impressive and illuminating narration of the *parousia* there is no reference to the punishment of the wicked or to hell. The concept of eternal suffering in the fires of hell was absent (2 Thessalonians 1.7-8) although St. Paul believes that a day of wrath will undoubtedly come (Romans 2.5, 8; 3.5; 5.9; 9.22) when vengeance will be exacted upon the unbelieving without him elaborating the nature of the divine vengeance and its duration. He only describes the heavenly beauty that awaits those who love God (1 Corinthians 2.9). Similar references are found in 1 Corinthians 15.23-24, which speaks about the resurrection of the faithful in the *parousia* and the turning of Christ's kingdom to God and the abolition of death.

Afterlife in the Gospels

It is only in the Synoptic Gospels and in James 3.6 that we see, for the first time in biblical literature, the concept of what is generally understood as hell, which is the translation of the Greek term *Gehenna*. In Mk 9.43, it is attributed to the lips of Jesus: "If your hand causes you to stumble, cut it off; it is better to enter life maimed than to have two hands and *go to hell to the unquenchable fire.*" Εις την γέενα, εις το πυρ το άσβεστον (*into hell, into the unquenchable fire*).

Such phrases accentuate the nature of *Gehenna*: it is now the 'fire of hell' or the 'unquenchable fire,' where 'their worm does not die, and the fire is not quenched' (v. 44). It asserts unambiguously that *Gehenna* will be a place of eternal punishment of outer darkness, where there will be weeping and gnashing of teeth.' (Matt. 25.46; Mk 9.48; cf. Isa 66.24; Mt 8.12).

However, this interpretation fails to convey both the nature of the punishment administered in hell and the temporal aspect of that punishment (how long it lasts). Nevertheless, one can infer from the description of hell as a place "where their worm never dies, and the fire is never quenched" (Mk 9.48) that *Gehenna* will be a location of eternal punishment. Elsewhere in the Gospels, *Gehenna* is consistently referred to as a place of punishment prepared for the wicked – comprising the Devil and his angels, hypocrites, the disobedient, and those who reject Jesus, God, or the prophets. Gehenna may be pre-existent (Mt. 25.41, where it has been 'prepared' beforehand), and its punishment is eternal (Mt. 25.41, 46); it serves as both the place of judgment for the souls of the wicked immediately after death (Lk. 12.5) and for the judgment of the wicked in a reunited body and soul after resurrection and judgment (Mt. 10.28). Predictably, its location is understood by Jesus to be in the depths of the earth. Finally, it appears that Jesus taught that hell would involve eternal, conscious punishment, with such images as the 'undying worm,' 'fire that is not extinguished,' and the emotive picture of 'weeping and gnashing of teeth' (Mt. 5.29-30).

This kind of imagery that describes hell originates from the Aramaic word *Gehenna*, a location outside Jerusalem that was initially a cultic shrine for human sacrifice and later became a city dump. Jeremiah cursed it, and Isaiah depicts it as the destination for those who rebel against God (Isa 66.24). The continuous burning of garbage made the valley synonymous with eternal fire. Consequently, Jesus, in the Synoptic Gospels, employs the term *Gehenna* to describe existence apart from or against God. It is portrayed as a place of unquenchable fire (Matt 5.22; 18.9; Mark 9.43) and a pit into which the wicked are cast (Matt 5.29; Mark 9.45-48; Luke 16.23). They provide a warning of what life apart from or against God may bring. Such language in this particular context is mainly figurative and parabolic because it deals with realities that lie far outside human experience. As such, it cannot be understood literally. The gospel of Jesus is primarily good news, the joyful announcement of the coming reign of God. His words about hell are not elaborated upon but serve chiefly to admonish the people to turn to God.

God's Universal Love and Desire for Salvation

Scripture conveys God's profound love for the entire world and His desire for all individuals to be saved. John 3.16 states, "For God so loved the world that He gave His one and only Son, that everyone who believes in Him shall not perish but have eternal life." This verse emphasizes the universality of God's love and the availability of salvation to "everyone who believes." Furthermore, 1 Timothy 2.3-4 affirms, "This is good and pleasing in the sight of God our Savior, who wants all people to be saved and to come to a knowledge of the truth." The apostle Paul highlights God's desire for all individuals to attain salvation and comprehend the truth of the Gospel. The promise of eternal life is a fundamental aspect of the salvation offered to all. Titus 2.11-13 states, "For the grace of God has appeared, bringing salvation to all people. It instructs us to renounce ungodliness and worldly passions and to live sensible, upright, and godly lives in the present age, as we await the blessed hope and glorious appearance of our great God and Savior, Jesus Christ." Thus, in the Christian tradition, we can recognize two seemingly incompatible views that resist reconciliation in an overall synthesis. The first warns us of the possibility of eternal damnation, while the second emphasizes God's will and power to save everyone (Acts 3.21; Rom. 11.25-32; 2 Cor. 15.24-28; Eph. 1.10; Phil. 2.10; 1 Tim. 2.4; 2 Peter 3.9).

St. Isaac the Syrian explicitly rejects the notion of a retributive God in his "Treatise on Gehenna." He argues that "love, a fundamental attribute of the Divine nature, is incompatible with a God who acts retributively." For St. Isaac, the concept of a retributive God is too human and unloving. He asserts that when it comes to love, it is not about requital, and vice versa. Therefore, the eternal torment of sinners does not align with the motive of Christ's Incarnation for St. Isaac.

In St. Isaac's view, God's ultimate revelation in Christ's life is characterized by mercy towards sinners. Instead of retribution, Christ sacrifices His life to offer forgiveness to the wicked. If God's ultimate attitude towards the wicked is eternal punishment, why provide a means of salvation through the incarnation at all? The incarnation of the Son of God and its impact on the world define paradise and hell not as places but as ways of being, modes of existence. These modes encompass living with God or lacking a relationship with Him. Their development begins in this life and continues after death. Essentially, the priorities, values, and relationships people have in this life grant them the potential to recognize and graciously continue living in communion with God, experiencing what the Church Fathers refer to as true life, αληθινή ζωή. Conversely, those who freely choose to live apart from God in this life would be unable to recognize and relate to Him, resulting in hell. Thus, as St. John of Damascus states, every person has the potential to live and be receptive to God's love, but some may choose not to commune with Him and start to experience their life as hell in this world and in the afterlife: "Participation in God is joy; non-participation in Him is hell." In his view, what a person desires in the last moments of life – either the good God or sin – is what will always accompany them, because from that point, the soul does not change. People who desire God, after death, continue to desire Him, since life is one, and they rejoice. In contrast, sinners, who constantly contemplate evil and sin, desire sin after death and are punished without any consolation, as they no longer have the means to sin. They have lost the material of sin, as he states, since they no longer possess their bodies and cannot sin, but their souls continue to crave only sin. "Therefore, those who desire and lack the things desired are burned by desire as by fire." For this reason, St. John of Damascus asserts that hell is nothing other than the deprivation of what is desired. Sinners, who choose sin yet lack its means, are tormented, as if seated beneath fire and worms, and find no comfort, while the righteous, who desire God and possess Him eternally, rejoice. For what is hell if not the deprivation of what is desired? (Τι γαρ εστί κόλασις ει μη του ποθούμενου στέρησις?) Thus, heaven and hell are purely matters of the will. According to the analogy of desire, those who desire God are happy, and those who desire sin are in hell.

In the writings of St. John of Damascus, hell is not an eternal punishment, but rather a deprivation of what is desired; it represents a failure of man's desire. The Devil and the damned yearn for non-existent things, as there is no evil and sin after death. However, desire persists and consumes man. Once the body is severed from human existence, man does not eat, marry, dress, become wealthy, feel envy, or engage in any form of sin. After death, there is complete reality, embodied by the good God, whom the damned reject. Consequently, desiring what they cannot attain, they are tormented by desire like a fire, while those who desire only God receive the blessing of living in eternal presence and communion with Him.

The possibility of hell for those who separate themselves from God through the choices they make is not denied. People, by choice, may stubbornly refuse to live with God, and this is the judgment they bring upon themselves – hell. As Metropolitan Kallistos Ware writes, quoting St. Isaac the Syrian, "Hell is not God's rejection of humankind but humankind's refusal of God. It is not a punishment God inflicts upon us, but a state of mind in which we punish ourselves. God does not shut the door against those in hell; He does not withdraw His love from them, but it is they who deliberately harden their hearts against that love."[1] Thus, the

---

1 Kalistos Ware, "Dare We Hope for the Salvation of All?" in *The Inner Kingdom*, (Crestwood, NY: 2000), p. 211.

biblical texts concerning the possibility of eternal suffering are "threat discourses," paraenetic, and admonitory, not predictions of coming events that justify hope for the universality of redemption. However, the possibility of eternal damnation also persists. In short, we must maintain side by side and unwaveringly the truth of the omnipotence of the universal salvific will of God, the redemption of all through Christ, the duty of all men to hope for salvation, and the possibility of eternal loss.

VIII

THE EXPERIENCE OF SALVATION

St. Paul, in his letters to Romans, proclaims that people receive salvation if they confess Jesus is the Lord and believe in their hearts that God raised him from the dead (Romans 10.9). Since the apostolic times, Christians believe in and worship Jesus Christ as the savior of the world. In proclaiming the Christian gospel, they proclaim to the world that through Christ's death and resurrection, a new age has dawned for the world.

But what is salvation? From what did Jesus save humans? Ordinary Christians tend to identify salvation with life after their physical death. They are willing to see this life as preparation for eternal life and life in paradise, and they strive to avoid the torments of hell in life after death by living a virtuous life. Does the Church's message about our salvation significantly affect people's lives in the present world? Do the people in the present world feel the need to be saved?

The need for salvation is intrinsically linked to how human alienation from God is understood and how people interpret their propensity to evil and its pervasiveness in the world. Thus, salvation directly relates to humanity's predicament and alienation from God. If people view their life apart from God as life in darkness, without value and a sense of direction, they understand salvation as illumination and enlightenment. Suppose they feel their lives have become captive to external forces, hostile to life powers, and have surrendered their existence to animal instincts of self-survival at all costs. In that case, they welcome salvation as liberation from the Devil, sin, and all the destructive forces and drives that may have the upper hand in their lives. If sin caused mortality, corruption, and death to God's creation, then salvation is perceived as deification in the sense of raising humanity to share in the life of God. Jesus Christ restores all creation to its authentic existence, which is realized as he makes possible the unity of all with God. The conviction that something is wrong with humans apart from God appears repeatedly in the New Testament. Jesus comes as the divine physician to cure sinners of their sickness (Mk. 2.17). Through sin, people become "heartless" (Rom. 1.31), closed in upon themselves, and thus incapable of love. Jesus declares how evil emerges from a wicked heart: "From within, out of the heart of man, come evil thoughts, fornication, theft, murder, adultery, coveting, wickedness, deceit, licentiousness, envy, slander, pride, foolishness. All these evil things come from within." (Mk. 7.21-23). Leaving unrestrained, the evil that exists "within" ultimately brings death to the world. Does the Orthodox Church provide a narrative of life that allows people to overcome the evil that exists "within" and in the world?

In Orthodox tradition, humans created by God in His image and likeness are created, finite, mortal beings. As created beings, they depend on God's gracious love for their existence. They cannot be reduced to self-referential, self-enclosed, or self-sufficient entities. Their existence is actualized as they relate to God, nature, and others. They are by nature "ecstatic," self-transcending, relational beings. They are in the process of becoming and participating in a movement of freedom toward communion. Such a movement is life-sustaining and life-transforming if it is not coercive but a free act of love. Being in communion presupposes freedom since there is no love without freedom. In Orthodox theology, freedom is a gift of God to humanity that defines and shapes human beings as being in God's image. Human persons, because they are free, have the potential to transcend the limitations of their nature and experience the fullness of their humanity in opening their existence to God and others. They are responsible for the nature and the quality of the relationships they are crafting when encountering others. At the same time, human beings are limited, conditioned, and restricted by the givenness of their existence (poor housing conditions, broken families, unemployment, advertising, the media, and their distinctive complexes and genes). Death and corruptibility are also an inescapable boundary to all possibilities of life, a constant marker of human finiteness. Thus, human beings live amid a reflexive and complex relationship between transcendence and finiteness. They are free but also limited.

The tension between transcendence and finiteness, freedom and limitations, possibilities and actualities generate anxiety. Most of the time, humans fail to balance the two poles of their existence, tipping over to one side at the expense of the other. Either they ignore their limits and posture as gods or give away their freedom and succumb like animals to the worldly forces that squeeze and determine them. However, the tension between transcendence and finiteness and the potential imbalances it generates only partially exhaust the possibilities of living the fullness of human life. Relying on human ideologies, actions, and deeds to sustain and realize human fulfillment has proved to be an illusion. Human actions and ideologies are necessary vehicles that allow us to move towards human fulfillment, but in themselves are not, and they do not warrant it. Absolute faith in human actions and ideologies as the only way to realize human fulfillment is demonic and idolatrous. They do not liberate humanity from the absurdities and the meaningless of life.

Human life flourishes through its enhancement by God's active and all-pervasive presence of God in the world. For Orthodoxy, the origins of all human alienation are in the separation of humanity from God. Life is shaped not only by natural forces and human actions but also through the active presence of God in it through Christ and the Holy Spirit. Their trusting relationship with God enables human beings to cope with the anxieties and adversities of life. Only God's direct and personal intervention can save humanity and the world from mortality and all oppressive and annihilating forces. Because of His loving nature, God grants the fullness of life as salvation from all deadly forces and realities through His incarnate Word and the Holy Spirit. It is God's will to save the world. Thus, whatever becomes an obstacle or ruptures a human being's communion with God and interrupts the process of attaining the fullness of their personhood is evil. Scripture portrays a diversity of forces, such as sin, death, the law, Satan, demons, principalities, and powers, that endanger our relationship with God and put at risk the quality of human life. The fact that men and women are oppressed, contaminated, and inwardly wounded should not be exaggerated to the point of alleging a complete lack of freedom, total corruption, and utter egocentrism. Evil spoils and damages but never destroys man's divine image. What was free, pure, and good in divine creation can never be erased.

St. John Chrysostom rightly points out that salvation, the fullness of life, comes "neither from God's love alone, nor just from human virtues, but from both together." If salvation were from God's love alone, then all would be saved, making human freedom superfluous; if it were from human virtue alone, there would have been no need for the incarnation. Making the right choices and living a virtuous life are not enough for human beings to attain the fullness of life. Human life depends on God's grace; thus, communion with God is indispensable to human flourishing. Such a pattern of life presupposes living virtuously. It implies that authentic human beings participate in and communicate the love of God for all human beings and the world.

IX

GOD'S PRESENCE IN
HUMAN SUFFERING

How we understand and experience communion with God differs in times of joy and suffering. While everything goes well in our lives, it is possible to acknowledge the thankfulness of God's blessings and benevolence in times of affliction and especially of undeserved suffering, people have difficulty discerning and experiencing the benevolent presence of God in their lives. They may even question His providence, love, and righteousness in such circumstances. Yet, it is also true in situations of suffering and affliction that people come to terms with their vulnerability and limitations and thus open themselves to God and others.

The very existence of every human being depends on the love that originates in God and is mediated by the love given to them by those who love them. Human flourishing is traumatized whenever the reflexive relationship between receiving and giving love is disrupted. Suffering and love are intrinsically related. One may argue that someone who has not suffered has never experienced what it is to love and to be loved. Suffering is an uninvited guest that affects our personal and communal life. The most severe form of suffering consists of relations violated, intimacy destroyed, in various states of alienation, betrayal, and abandonment.

The suffering that comes about because of the interpersonal nature of our existence takes two primary forms: affliction and tragedy. Pain has to do with the social nature of personhood. As social beings we depend on others for much of our identity; we are vulnerable to the fragility of social worlds. The need for social solidarity makes us vulnerable. Affliction involves abandonment and degradation or the fear of them in some form. The degradation is felt in the isolation that accompanies pain. The loss of solidarity experienced by the afflicted is a common phenomenon. Affliction is suffering that has at the same time, physical, psychological, and social elements. Suffering can also be tragic. The ancient Greek tragedians described the dynamic of tragic suffering against a background of the conflict, of forces beyond control. Love exists in a sad world where love and lovers are constantly threatened. All vulnerabilities, all losses, and all specific suffering are for the person's indications and symbolizations of the ultimate failure, which is death. This is the most tragic form of torture. No life can be managed to render it invulnerable to the anxiety engendered by the anticipation of death – of those we love and our own.

As we have presented, suffering is not something incidental or external to a person. Suffering enters the very texture of one's life journey. As a constitutive component of personal existence, a negative reality cannot easily be transformed into a positive one. No one can pretend to have ultimate answers to the why of suffering. There is a question of the intractability of suffering. The real anguish of suffering is found in its perceived meaning. There is so much innocent and pointless suffering that no straightforward interpretation is possible. History is a mixture of meaning and meaninglessness, sorrow and happiness. Such a mixture raises the question of whether, as a last resort, we can trust life.

The willingness to accept suffering to perfect one's personality is difficult to accept. Suffering is generally understood to have a negative value, an experience that inescapably diminishes human existence. But is suffering all bad? Is it always a net of loss, or can it sometimes be the occasion for real growth? Even though the best human creativity has been disclosed and expressed in situations of suffering, we cannot say, "Suffering is good for us." A surplus of suffering in the world cannot be of any value to anyone.

Faith in God addresses the meaning of "undeserved' human suffering in its task to interpret human existence. It communicates the belief that life is excellent and meaningful despite the suffering it entails. Suffering as a spiritual challenge refers not to ways to avoid suffering but how to suffer, how to make physical pain, personal loss, worldly defeat, or the helpless contemplation of other's agony something bearable or sufferable. Suffering in the Christian tradition has often been understood as a great teacher, as a source of wisdom and maturity. However, there are limits to perceiving suffering as a fundamental cause for promoting human maturation. Yet, all forms of Christian life must be grounded in a refusal to ignore suffering. For Christianity, Christ is the way, the model by which Christians give meaning to suffering. To suffer with Christ, the claim is made, transforming mere suffering into renewed trust in God and openness to the life-giving spirit.

Can suffering be the occasion for real growth? Spiritual writers and psychologists have used the term "false self" to suggest how illusory our self-image can be when aspects of the self are denied and repressed. In suffering, I am most alone. My suffering is exclusively mine: it bears my name as no other experience does because it seems to insulate me from others. This painful isolation gives access to the bottom depth of selfhood – the locus of transcendence – that can remain unsuspectingly hidden to the untroubled mind. Suffering makes us aware of the self's hidden depth and its insufficiency. Acceptance of suffering is an acceptance of that which exists. Denying every form of suffering can result in a flight from reality. To reject one's suffering marks the beginning of the loss of selfhood. The making of the self depends upon the self's courage to face the negativity of suffering fully. When fully met and accepted, suffering can be incorporated into the creativity of the self. Acceptance can be the most difficult and, simultaneously, the most crucial element of one's spiritual existence. Acceptance does not eliminate the negativity of suffering and transforms it into a positive reality.

Jesus' prayer in the Garden of Gethsemane shows a way to move from meaningless suffering to creative suffering. Acceptance of suffering is acceptance of a mystery that no logic can resolve.

Through this acceptance, we are set on the road to meaning. In the following Psalm, note the acceptance of suffering and the acceptance of mystery.

> Hasten to answer me, O Lord, for my spirit fails me.
> Hide not your face from me, Lest I become like those who go down to the pit.
> At dawn, let me hear of your kindness, for in you I trust.
> Please show me how I should walk, for I lift my soul to you.
> Rescue me from my enemies, O Lord, for in you I hope (Ps 143.7-9)

When Job listened to God in abandonment and solitude, he saw his place in the mystery of things:

> I know that you can do all things and that no purpose of yours can be hindered.
> I have dealt with things that I do not understand.
> Things too wonderful for me, which I cannot know.
> I had heard of you by word of mouth, but now my eye has seen you.
> Therefore, I disown what I have said and repent in dust and ashes. (Job 42.2-6).

In the journey of transcending, a person must finally arrive at the fundamental conclusion that God alone is God and that what counts ultimately is the love of God. When everything else goes, God alone remains; nothing is God but God. From early on, Christians have been aware that no suffering can separate us from God's love (Rom 8.38-39).

The French philosopher, mystic, and political activist Simone Adolphe Weil (1909–1943) is familiar with the consequences of affliction when it appears that God appears to be indifferent or not intervening or hearing the supplications of the victims of unjust and incomprehensible suffering and offers the following advice:

> The soul must go on loving in the emptiness, or at least to go on.
>
> She wanted to love, though it may only be with an infinitesimal part of herself. One day, God will come to show Himself to this soul and reveal the world's beauty to it, as in Job's case.

We must persist in loving and trusting God and hoping in situations of darkness and emptiness until God discloses the fullness of His love. Moments of affliction, without the presence of God as hope, are already the experience of hell.

X

JESUS AND THE
COMING REIGN OF GOD

The central message of the Christian Gospel is the proclamation of God's love, compassion, and care for all humanity and his determination to grant life in abundance to the world, inviting them into unity with Him. The New Testament communicates the faith of the early Christian community that God, in and through Jesus of Nazareth, has acted decisively for the world's salvation. The first three Gospels, the Synoptics, make it abundantly clear that at the heart of all that Jesus said and did lay what he called the coming reign of God. "After John was imprisoned, Jesus came into Galilee, *preaching the Gospel of the Kingdom of God* and saying that the time is fulfilled, and the Kingdom of God is at hand: repent and believe the Gospel." (Mk1.14-15 cf. Lk 8.1; Matt 4.23)

The expectation of God's imminent intervention into the world's life presupposed a particular understanding of humanity as incapable of transcending the limitation of its nature and being united with God, experiencing the fullness of its being. It is assumed that Human beings are captives of external forces, "demons," "principalities and powers of this age," who bring evil to the world by separating the world from God. The Bible shows that things that are created good can develop into powers hostile to themselves and the world. Against this background, it becomes apparent why a new, completely fresh start was necessary, a newness that only God, as the Lord of life and history, could give.

What did Jesus mean with His teachings about the coming of God's Kingdom? Jesus described and communicated that the reign of God came to the world through images, parables, and miracles. He assumed that His audience was familiar with the expectation of the coming reign of God. To be sure, Israel's people had different understandings of God's Kingdom at that time. The Pharisees understood it to be a complete fulfillment of the Torah; the Zealots envisioned a political theocracy, which would be installed by force of arms; and the Apocalyptics looked forward to a new realm of existence, a new eon, "the new heaven and new earth." All the different interpretations shared the belief, the hopeful expectation that God will visit His people, granting them the salvation that coincides with the establishment of the eschatological *shalom*, peace among nations, peace between individuals, peace within communities, and peace in the whole universe. To expect the Kingdom meant to be open to the coming of God and nothing less. It had universal significance, for when God comes, the world must change; things cannot remain as they are. The reign of God will end all resistance to God's rule and grant the gift of God's grace to those in need of a new beginning. What was distinctive in Jesus' message about the reign of God was the expectation that the Kingdom of God is close at hand; it is already arriving. However, the coming of God's reign began with Christ's ministry, death, and resurrection as a slow incremental process, a movement of entering God's realm (Kingdom). In one of his parables, Jesus compared the Kingdom to a mustard seed, proverbially known as the smallest of all seeds. With His customary hyperbole, Jesus said it grows into 'the greatest of all shrubs' with branches where birds can nest. In Jesus' teaching and activity, God sowed the seed of his coming Kingdom.

If the Kingdom's arrival was so unimpressive, why might it be recognized as the coming of God's Kingdom? The answer to this lies in Jesus' understanding of the character of the Kingdom. What is God's rule like? For Jesus, the reign of God becomes actively present in the world through His ministry that brings God's healing and forgiveness into the lives of people He met, reaching out to those who were pushed to the margins and gathering a community in which service would replace status. These are the sorts of things that happen when God rules. To his disciples, Jesus spoke of the extraordinary moment of history they were witnessing:

> Blessed are the eyes that see what you see! For I tell you that many prophets and kings desired to see what you see, but did not see it, and to hear what you hear but did not hear it. (Luke 10.23-24)

The Kingdom of God was coming because Jesus enacted it and proclaimed it. While Jesus did not provide a precise and exhaustive description of the nature of God's Kingdom, He offered a relative understanding of what the Kingdom of God is and how it is changing the world through stories, images, and miracles. Jesus, through His teaching parables, compares the Kingdom of God to a grain of mustard seed, out of which comes a great tree (cf. Mk. 4.30-2). He wished to communicate that in the most ordinary events of the present, whose real significance no one can easily discern without faith, that there is the Kingdom of God lies hidden.

Jesus rejects spectacular displays of power (Mt. 12.38-45; 16.1-2; Lk. 11.29-32; Mk. 8.11-12); His Gospel brings healing and love rather than a manipulative production of power. His miracles indicate that in and through his ministry, the new creation has dawned. They are deeds of divine power that express and proclaim love's victory over the demonic forces and the limits of the created nature. God saves humanity in their whole physical and spiritual reality.

In Christ's healing ministry, there is no planned or systematic attempt at improving the world. Jesus did not heal all the sick nor drive out all the demons; He gave signs, which are only understood within the context of His message of the coming Kingdom of God. His miracles were intensive, extraordinary manifestations of the divine presence. They symbolize anticipations and intimations of how God's final reign will affect people's lives. It was expected to provide the suffering people healing and holiness, liberation and reconciliation, and a new experience of the fullness of life. Their direct purpose, therefore, is not to illustrate something about Jesus but to embody the presence of the new community of love: "But if it is by the Spirit of God that I expel demons, then the reign of God has overtaken you" (Mt 12.28 cf. Lk 11.20).

An aspect that makes the Kingdom of God an elusive reality in Jesus' teaching is the tension between His present and future sayings. One set of sayings proclaims the Kingdom of God is here and now, whereas others speak of the Kingdom as something to be prayed for and awaited in the future. Thus, the Christian faith has kept these two truths tense since their early stages. It maintains that the Kingdom of God has already arrived in Christ while acknowledging that its full potential will be realized in the future. Thus, the transition from old to new age no longer lies in the unattainable future but is immediately at hand. "The time is fulfilled, and the Kingdom of God is at hand" (Mk. 1.14-15; Mt. 4.17; cf. Mk. 10.7; Lk. 10.9, 11). Jesus' life, teachings, and activities are decisive signs of God's final divine and saving intervention into the world's life (Mt. 12.28).

Did the Reign of God Come?

Jesus expected God to establish His rule's power and glory immediately. Instead, the world has gone on without fulfillment of this expectation. Was not Jesus, therefore, proved wrong by the ongoing course of history? Furthermore, Jesus, in His message, had aroused hope that God was coming soon in power and glory to end misery, poverty, and oppression, but instead, Jesus Himself was crucified. How does the Cross of Jesus relate to God's coming Kingdom? The Gospel writers interpreted Jesus' death and resurrection as the Kingdom's fulfillment. It was a fulfillment hidden under the sign of the Cross and, therefore, not manifest in all the power and glory that was expected. On the road to Emmaus, the disciples had sighed: "But we had hoped that he was the one to redeem Israel" (Lk. 24.21). But on the third day, stories began to circulate that the crucified Jesus had appeared to some of His friends and disciples. The first witnesses interpreted these appearances of the living Jesus as evidence that God had raised Jesus from the dead. Jesus' resurrection signified the eschaton's beginning in the middle of history. The lordship of Christ is hidden under the Cross, guided by the resurrection, alive in the Spirit, attested by faith, and at work through the Church in contesting the powers that still rage against the life and the future of God's creation. But what is now hidden in history will be unveiled in glory when the world finally reaches its fulfillment in the final manifestation of God's coming reign.

In the Christian tradition, the understanding of God's Kingdom has been reduced to that of an otherworldly reality, an inner spiritual condition, or an outward, social, and moral force. It has been suggested, for example, that the Kingdom of God is actualized in history wherever people live according to the ethical principles which Jesus taught, especially in the Sermon on the Mount. Such morality indeed befits the true nature of being human and being Christian. Biblical scholars have pointed out that the Kingdom of God in Jesus' preaching was mainly not a moral achievement but a gift of God. Jesus did not offer a direct formula for translating the Kingdom of God into an earthly situation. He did, however, present ethical teachings that must be understood as signs of the Kingdom's imminent coming and presence. That is to say, the Kingdom of God will not come as the cumulative result of good human works and historical progress. Instead, it is a miracle of God's power breaking in from beyond the realm of human potentiality. This view of history radically challenges the identification of God's Kingdom with utopias since the latter is an outcome of human imagination realized exclusively through human efforts. Such an understanding reduces the Kingdom of God to a human ideology and project, ignoring its dependence on God's compassion and love for His people.

XI

SUFFERING AND
THE CRUCIFIED CHRIST

Suffering is an inescapable aspect of human life in the present world. Suffering, affliction, and tragic experiences disclose the vulnerable nature of human life; they enable us to recognize our limitations and dependence upon others and God for sustenance in life. Suffering has the potential to lead human beings either to despair, misery, and self-enclosure or to transcendence through hope and faith, trusting the benevolence of God and His covenant relationship with His people.

Humans have a strong instinct to seek reason(s) for their suffering. Why? Why me? These questions emerge from every human experience of suffering. The need to search for the causes of suffering is deeply ingrained in us. Sometimes, we find the answer and modify our behavior in the light of bad experiences. But, sometimes, the causes are beyond our knowledge or control, and the search leads to increased frustration, misplaced guilt, or blaming others. Yet, we find it hard to accept that we may never know the real reason for our suffering. We resent the inexplicable mystery, especially when we feel helpless and numb in the face of meaningless suffering. Thus, our search for meaning and explanations employs all our rational capacities to find intelligible causes for the inexplicable.

Every act and reflection on suffering and death must begin by doing justice to the human experience. Not all suffering is meaningless. Suffering can be an opportunity for maturation, an occasion to direct one's life to the essentials. Nevertheless, the suffering often encountered is deadening, brutal, and meaningless. The experience of human suffering raises questions about its meaningfulness or, alternately, its meaninglessness. Suffering can never be kept at a distance: I am constantly involved in it; I share in it, either personally or insofar as I share in the lives of others.

Undeserved suffering makes suffering intolerable in a world that is not ruled by irrational fate but by the just and mighty God. In Scripture, we find multiple responses and interpretations of what suffering means in a theocentric structure of reality. All of them, however, are worth understanding and may help in dealing with our suffering and that of others. Yet, none of these approaches are entirely satisfactory when taken independently. Nevertheless, each is a helpful resource for coping with suffering since escaping from suffering as long as we live in history is impossible.

Suffering is not a problem but an unfathomable, theoretically incomprehensible mystery. We should not try to explain suffering or construct theories about the reasons for suffering in the world and systematic explanations that seek to reconcile innocent suffering with belief in a good and all-powerful God. The pervading presence of senseless suffering in the world falls outside the bounds of every sound system. Remember how Dostoyevsky, in his book *The Brothers Karamazov*, was horrified in contemplating the worldwide suffering, especially the suffering of the innocent and the little children. The only answer that Alyosha (representing Dostoyevsky's faith and attitude) can give is the image of the Crucified: He can pardon all; He can reconcile all, for He has measured the depth of our afflictions, of our loneliness, and our pain. In the Crucified Christ, God does not remain a distant spectator of the undeserving suffering of the innocent. Still, He participates in their suffering through the Cross, and plants hope in all afflicted persons' lives through the resurrection. When faced with the mystery of evil and suffering, Jesus, as the story of God, is the only adequate response. The human quest for meaning and hope in tragic situations of affliction draws from Christ's death and resurrection the power of life needed for sustenance. Thus, Christians do not argue against suffering but tell a story.

The Suffering of Jesus

The suffering and death of Jesus were the outcomes of his public ministry, preaching, and making present the reign of God. The death of Jesus cannot be seen as an isolated act of redemption detached from what transpired in His life. The crucifixion of Jesus was the intrinsic historical consequence of His message and lifestyle. The Cross is salvific only in light of what God has accomplished in the resurrection. The crucifixion of Jesus is the ultimate expression of human rejection of salvation offered by God through Christ. God, who, according to Leviticus, 'abominates human sacrifices' (Lev. 18.21–30; 20.1–5), did not put Jesus on the Cross. Human beings did that. Although God always comes in power, divine power knows no use of force, not even against those who had crucified Christ. But the kingdom of God still comes, despite human misuse of power and rejection of God's love.

The fact that Jesus, in the last supper with His disciples, offered the cup to His disciples for one last time, with the trust that he will drink it anew in the reign of God (Mk. 14.25), indicates Jesus' trust that his communion with God and his disciples was more substantial than death. Jesus' cry of abandonment: "My God, my God, why have you forsaken me," taken from the opening line of Psalm 22, should be interpreted in light of the entire psalm. Read as a whole, this psalm is a prayer of anguish and a confession of trust in God. It concludes with an expression of praise and thanksgiving for God's deliverance. These words reflect Jesus' persistent trust in God even amidst the experience of darkness and the apparent failure of his mission.

God does not intervene to save Jesus, nor does God abandon Jesus. Jesus's life ends with an open question to God. "My God, my God, why have you forsaken me?" God answers to the crucified Jesus by raising him from the dead and glorifying him. The resurrection signifies that God is present in the suffering of Jesus and every human person. If we speak of Jesus' real abandonment by God at Golgotha, it could lead to the mistaken impression that suffering human beings are also forsaken by God. Instead, we must speak of God as silently present to Jesus at this terrifying moment, just as God is silently present to all those who suffer. This silent presence of God to Jesus becomes manifest in the resurrection. The resurrection of Jesus confirms and completes all that Jesus was about in his life. The bottom line of the Christian faith is that God will be victorious over evil and suffering, as exhibited and affected in the death and resurrection of Jesus.

God's relation to suffering has practical consequences for the Christian life. It means that Christians are called to be people of memory and action. So, first, believers in Christ keep the memory of human suffering – the memory of the ongoing passion of humanity. Christians are summoned to live in solidarity with suffering people and to enable suppressed stories of suffering to be told, whether they be the stories of individuals in pain or stories of people who are victims of systematic oppression. Christians also remember another story – Jesus' life, death, and resurrection. The story of the passion of Christ, remembered and lived out, speaks to us about the benevolence of God, who overcame the death of Jesus in the resurrection and is on the move to overcome all evil and suffering. The story of Jesus assures us that entering communion with suffering people and acting to bring life out of death is what God is doing for all people. Being attentive and hearing the stories of the afflicted and oppressed people, responding to their needs with compassion, care, and love, and actively working against the causes of suffering provide opportunities to participate in God's mercy and become true icons of His presence in the world. As Christians, we see the presence of the suffering Christ in our suffering brethren.

XII

MY GOD, MY GOD,
WHY HAVE YOU FORSAKEN ME?

Jesus on the Cross cried to His Father, "My God, my God, why have you forsaken me?" (Matt. 27.46; Mk. 15.34). In his suffering, He felt that even God had abandoned Him. This feeling identifies the crucified Lord with the unjust suffering and affliction of righteous people who, amid their incomprehensible plight, God has abandoned them.

The crucified Jesus chose to urgently address in prayer His Father by reciting Psalm 22. The Psalm begins by expressing the wonder of why God abandoned the righteous sufferer. Verses 1–21a describe the debilitating conditions of a righteous person immensely suffering because God abandoned him. Still, despite the divine forsakenness, he acknowledges his dependence on God, the source of his life and well-being. Then, in verses 21b-31, after hearing the urgent petition of the righteous sufferer, God becomes once again present in his life, bringing his blessing and a new life. In Psalm 22, the early Church identifies the suffering of Jesus with verses 21b–31, and in the rest of the Psalm, the miracle of God's intervention by raising Jesus from the dead.

Since the crucified Jesus prayed to his Father by reciting Psalm 22, it would be instructive for us to study the Psalm and learn how to address God in times of suffering, hoping to feel His redemptive presence through the risen Christ.

Psalm 22 narrates the experiences of a forsaken, righteous, suffering person with an intimate relationship with God. He remembers with gratitude what God had done in the past for Israel and His people, including himself.

In your ancestors trusted.

They trusted, and you delivered them.

To you, they cried and were saved.

In you, they trusted and were not put to shame. (vs. 4-5)

But now, the Psalmist and the people of Israel are experiencing unjustifiable suffering and oppression and wonder why God has abandoned them, reducing life into unbearable and incomprehensible misery. The Psalmist portrays his condition of grief, helplessness, and complete social failure by using, in an extended narrative, three entirely different images of rapacious adversaries (vv. 12–13), personal, physical disintegration (vv. 14–15), and social treatment "as good as dead" (vv. 16–18).

The affliction that the people of Israel and the Psalmist are experiencing is attributed to God's absence from their lives. The Psalmist, with a sense of urgency, questions God why He has chosen not to be present in his life:

Why are you so far from helping me, from the words of my groaning? O my God, I cry by day, but you do not answer. and by night but find not rest." (v.1a-2)

Psalm 22 reflects the belief of the people of Israel that a serious, engaged petition can mobilize God to salvific action that He would not otherwise undertake. If God is reminded of what He has done in the past, He could be motivated to be once again actively present in the lives of His people and do what He has done for them in the past (v. 3-5). Asking for God's return and presence assumes that God's remoteness and detachment have permitted troubles to occupy the void left by His divine absence. So, if God comes near and is present, He will turn a circumstance of trouble into one of well-being.

Despite blaming God's absence from his life for the suffering that he is experiencing, the Psalmist acknowledges that he has nowhere to turn to for help except God. Only if God is present and active in his life can the spiraling experience of the forces of suffering and death be reversed. "But you, O Lord, do not be far away! O my help, come quickly to my aid! (v.19). He pleads: "Do not be far from me, for trouble is near, and there is no one to help" (v.11). God is the only one who can rescue him from his affliction. The Psalmist confesses that since his birth, his life has depended entirely on God for sustenance.

Suddenly, the Psalmist drastically changes his tone. Something decisive has happened. The Psalmist voices no more distress but only amazement and gratitude. God has become attentive to his plight. God's active presence creates a new situation that the Psalmist needs to share with his "brothers and sisters."

> I will tell of your name to my brothers and sisters.
>
> In the midst of the congregation, I will praise you:
>
> You who fear the Lord, praise him!...
>
> For he did not despise or abhor
>
> the affliction of the afflicted.
>
> he did not hide his face from me,
>
> but heard when I cried to him." (v 22-24)

Thus, the dramatic movement of the Psalm affirms God, who comes into circumstances of death and gives new life. Sorrow is turned to joy. Psalm 22 refuses to accept the present circumstances of suffering and proclaims that God, through His presence, can advance the well-being of His people. The survival and well-being of the world depend on God's providential active presence and care. The absence of God causes suffering; only God can reverse it through His presence. Suffering is fundamentally alien to God's intention for His people (Rev. 21.3-4).

XIII

THE DEATH AND
THE RESURRECTION OF JESUS

Jesus ended His earthly life on the Cross. He "uttered a loud cry and breathed His last" (Mk. 15.37). The Gospel of Mark gives us a relatively plain statement of Jesus' death with these words. He was executed as a political rebel, as the inscription on the Cross indicates. "The King of the Jews" (Mk.15.26). Crucifixion was a Roman form of execution mainly used for enslaved people. It was forbidden to crucify Roman citizens. Cicero says: "The idea of the cross should never come near the bodies of Roman citizens; it should never pass their thoughts, eyes or ears."

Did Jesus expect that He would suffer and die on the Cross? Jesus had probably considered a violent death because of His ministry, for anyone acting as He did to be prepared for extreme consequences. From the beginning of His ministry, He faced the charge of blasphemy (Mk. 2.7) and was accused of alliance with the Devil or magic (Mt. 12.24) and infringing the law of Sabbath (Mk. 2.23-24; Lk. 13.14-15). His enemies watched Him in order to find grounds for arresting Him (Mk. 3.2), and they tried to trap Him with trick questions (Mk. 12.13ff. 18ff; 28ff.). Thus, Jesus' death flowed naturally from His public activity. It was the inevitable result of fidelity to His preaching, given the failure of His message to win general acceptance. Jesus accepted His death as the most radical consequence of the message He had proclaimed and embodied in His deeds.

How does Jesus' mission relate to His death on the Cross? How could the kingdom of God come when the forces of this world put its precursor to death? Jesus' preaching and praxis are called into question. Yet, amid this dark and lonely experience of being crucified, Jesus trustingly surrenders Himself to God the Father.

Three days after His death, the disciples of Jesus proclaimed that God had raised him from the dead. On this matter, the New Testament speaks with a single voice; "This Jesus God raised, and of that we are all witness" (Acts 2.32). The Christian Gospel is disclosed in Christ's resurrection. "If Christ has not been raised, then our preaching is in vain, and your faith is in vain." (I Cor. 15.14; cf. 17.9). His rising from the dead does not mean returning to the old life. He does not return to decay or corruption (Acts 13.34): "For we know that Christ being raised from the dead will never die again; death no longer has dominion over Him... The life He lives, He lives to God" (Rom 6.9ff.). The resurrection is not a resumption of the old life but the beginning of new creation (cf. I Cor 15.42ff.).

The New Testament contains the stories about Christ's resurrection. The Easter kerygma of the early Church is revealed in brief, kerygmatic and liturgical formulations of belief. However, one of the earliest witnesses of Christ's resurrection is recorded in Cor. 15.3-8:

> For I transmitted to you as of first importance what I received: that Christ died for our sins according to the Scriptures; and that He was buried; and that He was raised on the third day according to the Scriptures; and He appeared: first to Cephas, then to the twelve; and then He appeared to more than 500 brethren at one time, of whom most remain alive until today, though some have fallen asleep. And He appeared: to James then to all the apostles; last of all, as to one irregularly born, He also appeared to me.

Although St. Paul wrote I Corinthians about 56 A.D., he tells the Corinthians (15.3) that what he transmitted to them (presumably when he first went to Corinth about 50 A.D.) was information that he had "received" at an earlier time (in the mid-30s).

The resurrection of the crucified Jesus is exclusively an act of God, for which no analogy happens in space and time. Consequently, it cannot be idealized, symbolized, or allegorized. Nevertheless, the effects of Jesus' resurrection – the faith that arose in His disciples, the formation of the Church, the continuity of His ministry by His disciples, and the descent of the spirit – are already signs of the "new creation," the inauguration of God's reign in the world.

The early Christians consider the death of Jesus to be a victory over the powers of darkness operative in this world. For St. Paul, the death of Christ frees us from sin (II Cor. 5.21), from the flesh (Rom. 8.3-8), from death (Rom. 6.1-10), and the Law (Gal. 3.10-13; 4.4-5). The Cross reveals God's unique power, wisdom, and love (I Cor. 1.24). In virtue of the Cross, God is shown to be most active and present in those situations where He, at least externally, appears to be inactive and absent. In the Cross, God is active and current amid extraordinary evil, suffering, and death – drawing good out of evil, salvation out of suffering, and new life out of death. No area of life falls outside the presence and activity of God. The death of Christ puts an end once and for all to the suggestion that God is indifferent to the pain and suffering of humanity. God revealed in the crucifixion of Jesus is the compassionate God Who is moved and touched by the suffering and death inflicted by society on Jesus. God, the Father, is not indifferent to the suffering and death of His Son.

The resurrection of Jesus has brought salvation to the world: "If you confess with your lips that Jesus is the Lord and believe in your heart that God raised Him from the dead, you will be saved" (Romans 10.9). Jesus is the first to be raised from the dead (Acts 26.23; I Cor. 15-20ff.; Col. 1.18). Jesus' resurrection is attributed directly to God (cf. I Cor. 6.14; Rom. 10.9; I Cor. 15.15; et al.):" [You] killed the Author of life, whom God raised from the dead" (3.15; cf. 2.23ff. 5.30). The raising of Jesus from the dead is an act of divine power, an act of "the working of His great might" (Eph. 1.19ff; cf. Col. 2.12), an act of His glory (Rom. 6.4), and His Spirit (Rom. 8.11; I Pet. 3.18). The resurrection reveals Who God is: the One Whose power embraces life and death, existence and non-existence. It shows the world's future according to God's love and will. Jesus is raised as the first fruits of those who have fallen asleep (I Cor. 15.20; Col. 1.18; Acts 26.23; cf. 3.15; Rev 1.17ff).

The resurrection of Jesus Christ has universal consequences and significance, for it is the prefiguration and afore glimpse of the new creation, the new world that God has desired and made possible through His love, the sending of His Son, and the Holy Spirit. This new creation, the active presence of God's kingdom in the world, is strongly determined by negating the negative and openness to positive development. The dissolution of the negative is described in Revelation 21.4, "God will wipe away every tear from their eyes, and death shall be no more, neither shall there be mourning nor crying nor pain anymore." The openness and the positive development come with the establishment of a new relation of God with the world and the total renewal of the world by God: "They shall be his people, and he, God with them, shall be their God... And he who sat upon the throne said, behold, I make all things new" (Rev. 21.3,5). Through Christ's resurrection, God gave the world a foretaste of God's reign and told us how the world would be when all united with the exalted Christ participated in God's glory,

XIV

THIS IS THE DAY
OF THE RESURRECTION!

"This is the day of resurrection, let us be *radiant* O people: Pascha, the Lord's Pascha. For Christ our God has passed us from death to life, and from earth to heaven, we who sing the song of victory" (Katavasia of Pascha)

The Orthodox Church at Easter night celebrates Christ's resurrection. His resurrection liberates humanity from death. *"Christ is risen from the dead, trampling down death by death, and to those in the tombs, He has granted life."*

While we celebrate the defeat of death through Christ's death and resurrection, humanity still experiences physical death, the separation of the soul from the body. If we continue to experience physical death, does this mean that Christ did not conquer death?

To understand how Christ liberated humanity from death, let us briefly reflect on what it means to be human and the purpose of why God created humanity (Adam and Eve). As created beings, humans are changeable; they have a beginning and are subject to growth, aging, and ultimately death. But God created humanity to live. The fullness of life is experienced only in unity with God, the source and the cause of life.

Humanity, however, turned to itself instead of developing and deepening its relationship with God; it became egocentric, and under the influence of the Devil, it glorified itself. The separation of humans from God made death the inevitable end of existence. In Orthodoxy, death is understood not as the separation of the soul from the body but primarily as the separation of humans from God, the source of life.

As created beings having a beginning and an end, humans have the potential to transcend the limitations of our created nature – death – only as they relate to God and live in unity with Him. The incarnation of God's Word is the event that unites humanity and creation with God. Being fully divine and human, Christ connects all creation with God through his humanity. The incarnate Word of God, Jesus Christ, participated voluntarily in our sinful human condition, although He was sinless. He participated and experienced every aspect of human life to liberate us from the consequences of our fallible nature. If God did not intervene for the world's salvation, then we could argue that God's plans for the world have been disrupted by the rebellious humanity that had chosen death instead of life. Furthermore, one could say that God's love for the world is conditional, and He abandoned His creation once humans rebelled against Him.

However, God, the source of life, has never abandoned His beloved creation and continuously provides opportunities for humanity to establish a life-giving relationship with Him. God communicates His boundless love and compassion for all creation through the humanity of Jesus, His suffering, and His crucifixion. By His death, Christ conquered death and abolished the Devil who had the power of death until then. In the words of the author of the Epistle to the Hebrews: "That through death he (Christ) might destroy him that had the power of death, that is, the Devil; And deliver them who through fear of death were all their lifetime subject to bondage" (Hebrews 2. 14-15). The crucified and risen Christ defeats death.

St. Paul clarifies that the resurrection of Christ ensures the resurrection of the dead. "For since we believe that Jesus died and rose again, even so, through Jesus, God will bring with him those who have fallen asleep" (Heb.4,14). To illustrate his point, he uses two theological motifs. First, the Adam–Christ: "For since by a man came death, by a man also came the resurrection of the dead. For as in Adam all die, so also in Christ all will be made alive" 15.21-22). The second motif he uses is this life's natural, earthly body and the heavenly body after death. He describes how the new body will replace the old one at the resurrection of the dead: "So also is the resurrection of the dead. It is sown a perishable body, raised an imperishable body; it is sown in dishonor, raised in glory; it is sown in weakness, raised in power; it is sown a natural body and raised a spiritual body. If there is a natural body, there is also a spiritual body" (15.42-44). Thus, while human beings continue to experience physical death, the separation of the soul from the body, Christians believe that this is not their death, the end of their existence, but a temporary experience of "falling asleep" until the *parousia*, the return of Christ. Through Christ's death and resurrection, humanity has been granted the privilege to live eternally in God's kingdom. The resurrection of Christ is "The feast of feasts" and "The festival of Festivals." It is the most decisive act of the liberation of humanity from the Devil's power and death.

XV

MEMORY AND HOPE

Unjustifiable suffering challenges people's faith in God's benevolence and righteousness. People have difficulties relating unjust suffering with belief in a compassionate and generous God. Some people get angry with God considering their suffering and cease to trust Him since they do not feel His righteous and providential presence in their lives. Believers seeking comfort and solace in times of need turn to God. The basis of their hope is their faith in Christ. Based on the remembrance of God's benevolence in creating, sustaining, redeeming, and sanctifying the world, they refuse to consider their present suffering condition as the ultimate and final experience of their life in the world. Instead, they hope because they trust God's actions in Jesus Christ. Their hope is not a vague emotional attitude of optimism that ignores historical experiences of suffering and affliction. Christians – having experienced God's benevolent presence in their lives and remembering His marvelous deeds of creating, sustaining, and redeeming the world – trust God. They are confident that He will continue to lead them through the travails of history to His Kingdom.

How do Christians cope with conditions of loss, drawing strength from their memory of God's mighty acts in the world's life? The suffering of Jesus and His crucifixion interpret peoples' lives in history, and His resurrection discloses God's ultimate justification of those who suffer unjustifiably in this life. The disciples of Jesus believed that He was the "Messiah/Christ," the very presence of God in history whose mission is to unite the world with God. His suffering and His humiliating death on the Cross were a numbing experience for them. It filled their hearts with fear and disappointment. How could he be the expected Messiah if his life ended on the Cross? The early Christians chose not to forget or abandon trust in God because of disappointed expectations. The direct response of God to the passion of Christ is His resurrection, which brings to the world a greater future. His disciples refused to forget the suffering, the crucifixion, and the death of Christ. His resurrection filled their hearts with a hope of a future that depends on God's love and compassion. The resurrection of Christ instills hope amid despair. Christians amid loss remembered that life consists of mighty acts of generosity and transformation on the part of God, exemplified in Christ's life, death, resurrection, and the sending of the Holy Spirit.

Memory Generates Hope

Christians affirm that God, who has done past acts of transformation and generosity, will continue to act in a compassionate and transformative way in the present and future. It is a fundamental and indispensable element of the Christian faith that the profound loss in the death of Jesus did not disrupt God's power and resolve in the world. Christ's resurrection defines how God is present and operates in history. Thus, the Church is a community of memory that experiences seasons of loss as seasons of passionate memory, remembering God's steadfast love (for His faithful love endures forever). Amidst suffering, affliction, and hopelessness, they declare the confidence that God will act on their behalf, as expressed in the book of Lamentations:

> The steadfast love of the Lord never ceases,
>
> his mercies never come to an end;
>
> they are new every morning;

great is your faithfulness.

The Lord is my portion, says my soul,

Therefore, I will hope in him (Lam 3.21-24).

Christians believe that the future is shaped not only by human efforts and the laws of nature but also by God's gracious transformative presence and acts, as it has been done in the past. God continues to do what God has always already done. Christians are convinced that Jesus, the crucified one who had healed the sick, had forgiven the guilty, and had raised the dead, would do more. The resurrection of Christ and the sending of the Holy Spirit communicate in the most robust possible way God's determination to grant the world a future beyond the travails of history. The Easter event embodies God's power and the gift of the new creation that He grants to the world. Paul, in his Letter to the Romans, articulates a life of faith amid suffering:

> We boast in our sufferings, knowing that suffering produces endurance, and endurance produces character, and character produces hope, and hope does not disappoint us, because God's love has been poured into our hearts through the Holy Spirit that has been given to us (Rom 5.3-5).

Christians, remembering what God has done for the world's salvation, refuse to give in. God has not finished His work in the world. Their remembrance signifies that things are not yet finished for the disciples of Christ, and God must complete the future that is now beginning. The capacity to turn memory into hope during loss and suffering is not a psychological trick. Instead, it is a statement about the fidelity of God, a crucial factor in our past and future. Christian hope is grounded in the reality of God, who will and does work newness. Christian hope is for those who believe in Christ and the whole world. The Gospel affirms that in Jesus of Nazareth, God's reign for the creation has begun in a new way. This hope reaches the world through lovingkindness, compassion, and faith practices. In the New Testament, the Church's central claim is that Christ's spirit is at work to bring God's rule among us. The coming of God's reign, according to Jesus, will come suddenly:

> Therefore, keep awake, for you do not know when the master of the house will come, in the evening, or at midnight, or cockcrow, or dawn, or else he may find you asleep when he comes suddenly. And what I say to you, I say to all: Keep awake. (Mark 13.35- 37).

Amid personal and communal affliction, suffering, and tribulations, the Church hopes that God has intervened to grant us abundant life. This intervention of God on behalf of His beloved creation and the suffering humanity is considered a gift that admits that things are beyond people's control, but, in the end, everything will turn out to be good. Therefore, in faithfulness to God's love and compassion, people should look beyond their present conditions because, in the end, the future belongs to God (Eph 3.20-21).

XVI

THE CHRISTIAN VOCATION
OF BEING CHARITABLE

The vocation of every Christian and person of goodwill is to lessen the evil and suffering in the world. In the biblical tradition, the marginal groups in society – the poor, the widows, the orphans, the elderly, the disabled, the ailing, and the suffering – are the scales on which society's justice is weighed.

Jesus Christ, in his teaching ministry, had juxtaposed, as it can be found in Matthew 22.39 and Mark 12.31, the demand of loving God with all one's heart (Deut. 6.5) with the command to love one's neighbor as oneself (Lev. 19.18). He asked us to understand each command by considering the other. St. Paul wrote to the Galatians: "Through love be servants of one another. For the whole law is fulfilled in one word, 'you shall love your neighbor as yourself'" (Gal 5.13-14). The way that we love our neighbor reveals the authenticity of our faith in God in the most concrete terms (1 John 3.16-18). Faith demands an active love toward the poor and the needy (James 2.15-17). St. Gregory of Nazianzus unequivocally stated that salvation depends on loving and showing humanity to the sick and poor: "We should fix in our minds the thought that the salvation of our bodies and souls depends on this: that we should love and show humanity to these (the suffering poor)."

Charity and compassion are not virtues that only the wealthy must practice. It is the vocation that all people, even the poor, should practice:

> Are you poor? There is someone much more flawed than you are.
> You have enough bread for ten days; another has enough for one.
> As a good and kindhearted person, distribute your surplus equally
> to the needy. Do not shrink from giving of the little you have; do
> not treat your calamity as if it is worse than the joint suffering...
> Believe in the one who always takes up the cause of the afflicted
> in his person and supplies grace from his store.[1]

This cheerful compassion and giving are grounded upon the belief that "in nothing do we draw so close to God as in doing good to man."

The pastoral nature of the Church's faith did not allow the issue of poverty in situations of famine, homelessness, and sickness to be simply an issue of theological speculation. The Church urged the faithful to be compassionate and use their resources to manifest their faith in God. St. Gregory of Nazianzus implored his audience: "Let nothing come between your will and the deed. This alone must suffer, not delay kindness to another person ... a kindness done promptly is a kindness twice done. A favor done in a sour spirit, and because you must, is unlovely and without grace. We should be cheerful, not grieving, when we give mercy."

Identification of Christ with the Poor

The work of God's Spirit realizes our unity and communion with God. This communion is sustained, nourished, and actualized in history by hearing and proclaiming God's word, celebrating the Holy Eucharist, and a life of active compassion and care toward the poor and the needy. These three sacramental modes of being in communion with God, as interdependent notions, cannot be separated without distorting the ethos and the identity of Christian ethos.

Based on Matthew 25.31-46, Christians believe Christ is mysteriously present in the poor and the needy. St. Gregory of Nyssa reminds the rich that they must recognize the identity of the

---

1 Basil, *Tempore Famis et Citatis*, PG 31.320-321.

poor with Christ and acknowledge their unique dignity and role in the Christian community.

> Do not despise these men in their abjection; do not think them of no account. Reflect on what they are, and you will understand their dignity; they have taken the person of our Savior upon them. For he, the compassionate has lent them his person to bash the unmerciful and the haters of the poor… The poor are the treasures of the good things that we look for, the keepers of the gates of the Kingdom, opening them to the merciful and shutting them on the harsh and uncharitable. They are strongest of accusers, the best of defenders – not that they accuse in or defend them in words, but that the Lord beholds what is done toward them, and every deed cries louder than a herald to his who searches all hearts.[2]

The poor in St. John Chrysostom become the liturgical images of the holiest elements in all Christian worship: the altar and the body of Christ. Based on this sacramental identification of Christ with the poor, St. John Chrysostom suggests specific ways to express the recognition that Christ lives and is actively present in the poor and needy people:

> Do you wish to pay homage to Christ's body? Then do not neglect him when he is naked. At the same time that you honor him here [in Church] with hangings made of silk, do not ignore him outside when he perishes from cold and nakedness. The One who said, "This is my body," … also said, "When I was hungry, you gave me nothing to eat."[3]

So convinced is St. John of Christ's identity with the poor that he does not hesitate to put words in the mouth of Christ:

> It is such a small thing; I beg … nothing costly … bread, a roof, words of comfort. [If the rewards I promised to hold no appeal for you] then show at least a natural compassion when you see me naked and remember the nakedness I endured for you on the

---

2 Walter Shewring, Rich and Poor in Christian Tradition (London, 1948) p. 65
3 On Matthew, Homily 50.4.

cross … I fasted for you then and suffer hunger for you now; I was thirsty when I hung on the cross, and I thirst still in the poor, in both ways, to draw you to myself and make you humane for your salvation.[4]

---

4   Quoted by W. J. Burghardt, "The Body of Christ: Patristic Insights," in R. S. Pelton, ed., *The Church as the Body of Christ* (South Bend, Ind., 1963), p. 97.

XVII

ENTERING GOD'S KINGDOM:
REDEMPTIVE ALMSGIVING

This article will briefly study some aspects of early Christianity's developing conception of 'entrance requirements' for the Kingdom of God.

The economic status of the individual was, at one time, a condition that either guaranteed or virtually prohibited entrance into the kingdom (Lk 6.20; Jas 2.5; Mk 10.25). Furthermore, there was a debate in the early Church whether baptism guarantees entrance into the Kingdom (cf. Jn 3.5; Herm. Sim. 9.16. 1-4), or whether individuals' subsequent conduct (or misconduct) could jeopardize their inheritance.[1] This is the apparent context of the caution in Barnabas: "Let us never rest as though we were called and slumber in our sins, lest the wicked ruler gain power over us and thrust us out from the kingdom of the Lord' (4.13).

The tension is apparent even in the New Testament writings. On the one hand, the tradition despairs of human effort, maintaining that it is possible to enter the kingdom only by God's power; yet, on the other hand, early Christianity demands a high standard of personal 'righteousness' and virtue that will merit entrance into the kingdom. The latter is expressed by St. John Chrysostom in his *Homilies on the Gospel of St. John:* "it is impossible, though we perform

---

1 For the importance of good works as an entrance requirement of the kingdom, see 1 Cor. 6.9-10; Gal. 5.5:19-21; Mt 25.31-46; Herm. Sim. 9.13.1-3; 9.15.1-3; 9.29.1-2).

ten thousand other good deeds, to enter the portals of the kingdom without almsgiving." Chrysostom further claims that while baptism provides the initial cleansing from sin, almsgiving is the foremost means of 'wiping off the filthiness' of post-baptismal sin. Here we have a clear articulation of the doctrine of redemptive almsgiving, that almsgiving not only wins favor with God, earning the individual entrance into the kingdom of God, but even merits the forgiveness of sin.

How and why did early Christianity come to adopt a doctrine of almsgiving? A tradition that once ridiculed the idea that a wealthy man could enter the kingdom of God (Mk. 10.25; cf. Lk. 12.32-33) came to regard wealth as a blessing, a potential means of redemption: "He has made you rich, that you may assist the needy, that you have release of your own sins, by liberality to others. He has given you money, not that you may shut it up for your destruction, but that you may pour it forth for your salvation."[2]

The early Christian belief that Jesus's death is the unique atonement for sin seems incompatible with the doctrine of redemptive almsgiving. The two interpretations collide.

> For what else could cover our sins but his righteousness? In whom was it possible for us, in our wickedness and impiety, to be made just, except in the son of God alone? O the sweet exchange, O the inscrutable creation, O the unexpected benefits, that the wickedness of many should be concealed in the one righteous, and the righteousness of the one should make righteous many wicked![3]

> O splendid trading! O divine business! You buy incorruption with money. You give the perishing things of the world and receive in exchange for them an eternal abode in heaven. Set sail, rich man, for this market, if you are wise. Compass the whole earth if need be. Spare not dangers or toils, that here you may buy a heavenly kingdom.[4]

---

2 Chrysostom, 'On the Statues," Homily 2:18-20.
3 *Epistle to Diognetus*, 9:3-5.
4 Clement of Alexandria, *Rich Man* 32. Cf. G. E. M. de Ste. Croix's description of

The New Testament provides a foundation for both these interpretations; the former particularly evident in Hebrews and the letters of Paul while the latter is implicit in the teachings of Jesus and other New Testament traditions. The clear emergence of the doctrine of redemptive almsgiving in the Apostolic Fathers is partly to be explained by texts such as 1 Pet. 4.8 but certain identifiable social and theological issues promoted the doctrine so as to raise doubts about the all-sufficiency of Christ's death as an atonement for sin.

The Problem

The so-called Epistle to the Hebrews boldly expresses the belief of early Christianity that the death of Jesus provided an abiding sacrifice for sin that made the cultic ritual of Judaism obsolete.

> But in these sacrifices there is a reminder of sin year after year. For it is impossible that the blood of bulls and goats take away sins (10.3-4)...When Christ appear as a high priest...he entered once for all (ἐφάπαξ) into the Holy Place, taking not the blood of goats and calves but his own blood, thus securing an eternal redemption (αἰωνίαν λύτρωσιν, 9.11-12)...And every priest stands daily at his service, offering repeatedly the same sacrifices which can never take away sins. But when Christ had offered for all time a single sacrifice for sins he sat down at the right hand of God...For by single offering he has perfected for all time (μια γάρ προσφορά τετελείωκεν εἰς τὸ διηνεκές) those who are sanctified (10.11, 12,14).

The author goes on to claim that the prophetic vision of Jeremiah has been fulfilled in the new covenant (cf. Heb. 8.7-13) and he draws specific attention to the Lord's promise. 'I will remember their sins and misdeeds no more' (10.15-17). The significant claim is then made: 'there is no longer any offering for sin' (10.18) While such conclusion is theologically consistent, it has promoted an

---

this passage: "Clement puts most eloquently the argument that almsgiving and actually purchase salvation," In *The Class Struggle in the Ancient Greek World* (London: Gerald Duckworth, 1981), p. 435.

intolerance and hopelessness for Christians who were guilty of post-baptismal sin (Heb. 10.26-29; cf. 6.4-6; Herm. Man 4.3.1-2.).

The dominant, though not exclusive, New Testament view of the death of Jesus is in harmony with the letter to the Hebrews. According to 1 Corinthians, Paul maintains that it is of high priority for the Gospel that 'Christ died for our sins' (15.3). Elsewhere Paul argued that if justification were possible by any other means, including the Law, then Christ's death served no purpose (Gal. 2.21). Martin Hengel has recognized here "a fundamental break with the atoning and saving significance of sacrifice in the worship of the Temple in Jerusalem." Early Christianity has the 'revolutionary insight' that the crucified Messiah had borne the curse of the Law, offering himself as the ultimate sacrifice for sins: "The death of the Messiah Jesus on Golgotha had brought once and for all ... universal atonement for all guilt."[5]

The belief prevailed in the rabbinic literature, especially after the destruction of the Temple in 70 CE, that giving money to the poor or works of loving-kindness atone sin.[6]

This idea is implicit in the New Testament, but it is the Apostolic Fathers who boldly advocate a second means of redemption; almsgiving provides a ransom for sin:

> Almsgiving is therefore good as repentance from sin. Fasting is better than prayer, but almsgiving is better than both. Love covers a multitude of sins but prayer from a good conscience rescues from death. Blessed is every man who is found full of these things for almsgiving lightens sin.[7]

---

5 M. Hengel, *The Atonement* (Philadelphia: Fortress Press, 1981), pp. 44, 47. There are several passages in the New Testament writings that claim the death - indeed the very blood - of Christ has redeemed and secured the forgiveness of those who believe (cf. Mt 26.27-28; Eph. 1.7-8; I Pet. 1.18-19), even the whole world (1 Jn 2.2).
6 J. Neusner, *Judaism in the Beginning of Christianity* (Philadelphia: Fortress Press, 1984), pp. 95-99; also, A. Cronbach, *Philanthropy in Rabbinic Literature* (Cincinnati: UAHC, 1939), p. 6.
7 2 Clem. 16.4.

Do not be one who stretches out his hands to receive but shuts them when it comes to giving. Of whatever you have gained by your hands, you shall give a ransom for your sins.[8]

You shall remember the day of judgment day and night and you shall seek the face of the saints either laboring by speech and going out to exhort, and striving to save souls by the world, or working with your hands for the ransom of your sins. You shall not hesitate to give and when you give you shall not grumble…[9].

These texts from the period 70-135 CE raise the important question: How and why early Christianity came to hold and endorse a belief in redemptive almsgiving? Both the New Testament and the Apostolic Fathers maintain that Jesus Christ suffered "for us," that he died "for our sins," and that this sacrifice was sufficient to redeem humanity. From a theological standpoint, then, an early Christian appeal to almsgiving as a further offering for sin is not only unexpected, but it also seems to be virtual denial that the death of Jesus has made full atonement for sins. To regard almsgiving as redemptive is to grant considerable theological prestige to this specific act of charity. Why is redemption promised to the one who gives alms? Why is this offered as motivation?

Early Christianity holds incompatible views on wealth. Within the New Testament there is an utter rejection of those who are wealthy: "Woe to you that are rich for you have received your consolation" (Lk. 6.24). Yet the New Testament reveals a clear attempt to accommodate the wealthy. In 1 Timothy 6.17-19 the author warns that rich Christians are not to be haughty (υψηλοφρονείν) nor to build their hopes on wealth. Rather, they are encouraged "to do good, to be rich in good deeds, liberal and generous, thus laying up for themselves a good foundation for the future so that they may take hold of the life which is life indeed."

Hengel finds the roots of this 'religious justification' of the use of property in both Stoic and Jewish teaching, the latter being based

---

8 Did. 4.5-6.
9 (Barn. 19.10)

on the principle that "all good gifts come from God himself."[10] It is equally possible, however, to discern a development that is open to sociological analysis.

> The attitude of the Jesus movement to possessions and riches was ambivalent. One the one hand there was criticism of riches, and on the other the movement profited from them…This ambivalence can be seen as a sign of the lack of principle in the Jesus movement: renunciation of riches was not an essential condition of salvation, but it could be required in particular instances. This position can also be derived from the social situation of the Jesus movement: wandering charismatics without possessions could make a credible condemnation of riches; but as charismatic beggars they were also concerned that they should have their share of the produce of the land. The two things went well together. The generosity of many rich people could be encouraged by playing on their consciences over their riches. In any case these were the hated rich, tax-collectors, prostitutes, outsiders whose riches had gained by questionable means. Of course, their generosity also benefited the poor. [11]

Theissen's reference to the wealthy as a despised and dishonest group is an unwarranted generalization but his comments are nevertheless suggestive. The poor, even as they might criticize wealth, were in fact dependent on the continued affluence and generosity of the rich. Understandably, the poor might attempt to motivate charity. The wealthy on their part, in the face of criticism of their possessions (whether they were obtained honestly or not) might seek to justify their continuing financial security. Redemptive almsgiving could be advocated by the poor hoping to prompt charity, or it might be promoted by the wealthy attempting to rationalize their bounty as an invested treasury for the poor. Indeed, such a

---

10 M. Hengel, *Property and Riches in the Early Church* (Philadelphia: Fortress Press, 1974), p. 20.
11 G. Theissen, *The Sociology of Early Palestinian Christianity* (Philadelphia: Fortress Press, 1978), pp. 37-39.

doctrine could well have had the support of both rich and poor Christians. Evidence for an emerging attitude which reflected both the concerns of the needy and the interests of the wealthy is found in the Shepherd of Hermas.[12]

> Instead of lands, purchase afflicted souls, as each is able, and look after widows and orphans. Do not despise them… For this reason the Master made you rich… Blessed are they who are wealthy and understand their riches are from the Lord, for he who understands this will also be able to do good service.

---

12   Herm. Sim. 1.8-9; 2.10. See C. Osiek, *Rich and Poor in the Shepherd of Hermas* (Washington, DC: Catholic Biblical Association of America, 1983).

XVIII

THE UNIVERSAL JUDGMENT

(MATTHEW 25.31-46)

In the Hebrew Bible and the New Testament, there is a belief about the universal final judgment of God's people and the nations. A detailed exposition of the world judgment is given in Matthew 25.31-46. The judgment is held by the Son of Man (Matthew 25.31), who is identified with the exalted Christ, the Messianic shepherd and King (Matthew 25.32, 34), the Son of the Father (Matthew 25.34), and exalted Lord (Matthew 37.44), the eschatological Judge. The Judge is presented as a shepherd, just as in the Hebrew Bible, God is a shepherd (Ps. 23). Sheep and goats are separated. Right and left define blessing and damnation, respectively. Judgment is held over all human beings of all times, Jews and Gentiles alike. In the discourses of judgment, what God expects from those with whom he has established a covenantal relationship is communicated in the strongest possible tone. They are called to be faithful to God's will, as it is disclosed in the history of Israel and most especially in the teachings and life patterns of Jesus Christ.

Jesus Christ, in his teaching ministry, juxtaposes the demand of loving God with all one's heart (Deut. 6.5) with the command to love one's neighbor as oneself (Lev. 19.18). By placing these two commands in immediate juxtaposition Jesus asks us to understand each considering the other. This is a consistent trend in the gospels and even in St. Paul, who writes to Galatians: "Through love be servants of one another. For the whole law is fulfilled in one word, 'you shall love your neighbor as yourself" (Gal. 5.13-14). The ways we love our neighbor reveal the authenticity of our faith in God (1 John 3.16-18).

In the story of the last judgment, the exalted Lord, the shepherd, the Son of the Father, is identified with the hungry, the thirsty, the strangers, the naked, the sick, and the prisoners of all times and all nations. He bestows dignity to the destitute and marginal people by giving himself to them and being unreservedly identified with them. "Truly, I tell you, just as you did it to one of the least of these members of my family, you did it to me." In word and deed, Jesus takes to himself in a very special way the ill and the sinners, the despised and the abandoned, and treats them as his equals, making their cause his own. So, too, he says now that whatever was done to the helpless was done to him. Faith demands an active love towards the poor and the needy (James 2.15-17).

St. Gregory of Nyssa, a theologian and a saint of the undivided Church, exhorts Christians to recognize Christ's identification with the poor and acknowledge their dignity.

> Do not despise these men in their abjection; do not think them of no account. Reflect what they are, and you will understand their dignity; they have taken the person of our Savior upon them. For he, the compassionate, has lent them his own person to abash the unmerciful and the haters of the poor.[1]

For St. John Chrysostom, another saint and great preacher of the Word of God of the undivided Church, the poor are liturgical images of the most holy elements in Christian worship: the altar and the body of Christ.

> Do you wish to see his altar?... This altar is composed of the very members of Christ, and the body of the Lord becomes your altar... venerable because it is Christ's body... This altar you can see lying everywhere, in the alleys and the agoras, and you can

---

1 Love of the Poor; Walter Shewring, *Rich and Poor in Christian Tradition* (London, 1948), p. 65.

sacrifice upon it anytime… invoke the spirit not with words, but with deeds.[2]

To those who desire to pay homage to Christ, he gives the following advice:

Do you really wish to pay homage to Christ's body? Then do not neglect him when he is naked. While you honor him here [in Church] with hangings made of silk, do not ignore him outside when he perishes from cold and nakedness. For the One who said, "This is my body"… also said, "When I was hungry, you gave me nothing to eat."… Your brother is more truly his temple than any Church building.[3]

The underlying theological assumption for the active concern for those suffering is the belief that all people created by God constitute an inextricable unity, and salvation depends partly on how we relate to the suffering brethren. In the words of St. Gregory of Nazianzus:

We are all one in the Lord, rich and poor, bond or free, sound or sick; and one is the Head of all, He from whom are all things, namely Christ. And what our members are to each other, each of us is to the other, and all…We should fix in our minds the thought that the salvation of our bodies and souls depends on this. that we should love and show humanity to these (the suffering poor).[4]

Solidarity and compassion are virtues that all Christians should practice regardless of their possessions as signs of their Christian discipleship. The final universal judgment and how it has been received in the early Christian traditions seems to suggest that charitable action and sympathy for one's fellow man is the sole essence of Christianity. Is Christianity simply humanitarianism?

---

2 *Epistulam 2 ad Corinthios, Homilia* 20:3.

3 *On Matthew; Homily* 50:4

4 Gregory of Nanzianzus, Or. 43, De Pauperum Amore), PG 35 857-909. English Translation, M.F.Toal, *The Sunday Sermons of the Great Fathers* (Chicago: Henry Regnery, 1963) vol. 4, p. 56.

There is no doubt that according to the New Testament, humanitarian conduct is an essential condition of the gospel. But the commandment of love is a new commandment (John 13.34), because it has its basis and possibility in the revelation of God's love for all human beings in Christ.

Living in communion with God is sustained, nourished, and actualized in the Church by hearing and proclaiming God's word, celebrating the Holy Eucharist, and a life of active compassion and care towards the poor and the needy. Theological sensibilities and contextual realities in shaping the ethos of the Churches in history have contributed to giving primary emphasis in their lives on one of these three but equally important ways to be with God (Liturgy, Scripture, serving the poor). They consider one of them as more important in constituting their identity without dismissing the importance of the other two and their inextricable relation to one another. These three modes of communion with God, as interdependent notions, cannot be separated without distorting the ethos and the identity of Christian ethos. Furthermore, I suggest that Scripture, Liturgy, and caring for the poor should be understood to be equally important in constituting the ethos of the Church. Whenever one of these constitutive aspects of the Christian ethos is not adequately acknowledged and cultivated, the life and the witness but also the unity of the Christian Church suffers.

Caring for the stateless, the refugees, the children with no identity and protection, and the marginal people generally is, in my judgment, a sacramental act that unites Christians with God since He has been identified with them and demands that people should serve Him with acts of Justice, compassion, and care. He is with them as He is in the Liturgy as well as in the proclamation of the Christian Gospel.

XIX

FALLING IN LOVE WITH CHRIST

For the Orthodox Church, the authenticity of human life is realized in a living relationship with God through Christ and the Holy Spirit that enables humans to experience the fullness of their humanity in loving one another and serving those in need. Through their identification with Christ, Christians are signs of His living presence and action in the world. However, not all their actions reflect the presence of Christ in them. Evil and sin disrupt people's unity and identification with Christ.

The consumer mentality and the prevailing utilitarianism reduce relations to commodities people use for instant gratification, serving their self-interests. This mentality has influenced how some Christians understand their relation to Christ and others. They only refer to Christ if needed and selectively remember whatever from His teaching serves their self-interests. In the same spirit, others see Christ as an ethical teacher who taught us to love one another. While it is true that Christ, in His ministry, reveals through His pattern of life and His teaching the will of God, what Christ has granted to the world is much more than His ethical teaching. Still, others reduce their faith to an ideology that legitimizes their cultural identity, forgetting that Christ came to the world proclaiming the good news of the coming Kingdom of God, which is not of this world. Although these understandings clarify aspects of Christ's identity and relation to the world, they do not communicate the richness of the inexhaustible mystery of God's involvement in the world's life. Thus, reflecting on the relationship Christians should have with

Christ, their Lord and Savior, is essential.

For Orthodox Christianity, Jesus Christ is the very presence of God in the world that has come to grant us the fullness of life, which is defined as a divine-human reality. He is not just the presence of God in the world but also the revelation of what it means to be fully human since the fullness of our humanity is a theanthropic reality, a divine and human event.

In this short article, I will present St. Porphyrios's view that Christians should fall in love with Christ; their relationship with Him should be understood as erotic. "Our relation to Christ is love, eros, passion, enthusiasm, longing for the divine. Christ is everything. He is our love. He is the object of our desire."[1] St. Porphyrios elucidates the importance of this erotic love for Christ by describing the intensity of love a person has for his beloved. "If you are in love, you can live amid the hustle and bustle of the city center and not be aware that you are in the city center. You see neither cars nor people nor anything else. Within yourself, you are with the person you love. You experience her, delight in her, and she inspires you." He then raises the question: "Are these things not true? Imagine that the person you love is Christ. Christ is in your mind; Christ is in your heart. Christ is in your whole being. Christ is everywhere."[2]

Falling in love with Christ means we seek His attention however minimal it may seem to us sometimes. We must be thankful and appreciative of whatever blessings He bestows on us: "Let Him give us whatever He wishes... My Christ, whatever Your love dictates, it is sufficient for me to live within Your love." Those who live in and with Christ become divinely intoxicated. Joy fills their hearts since Christ is in himself joy. He is the all-joyful joy that surpasses every joy. This joy never fades away; it lasts forever. It is a gift of Christ, "who desires and delights in enriching our lives with joy." We know Christ through the joy that He bestows on our lives. It is primarily a

---

1   Elder Porphyrios, *Wounded by Love* (Limni, Evia: Holy Convent Chrysopigi, 2005) p. 96
2   Ibid, p. 97.

gift of His love for us that we graciously receive. For St. Porphyrios, the aim of life is "love for Christ, for the Church, for our neighbor." He states that "Love, worship of, and craving for God, the union with Christ and with the Church is Paradise on earth. Love towards everyone, Christ, and towards one's neighbor, towards everyone including enemies. The Christian feels for everyone, he wants all to be saved, all to taste the kingdom of God. That is Christianity: through love for our brother to arrive at love for God. To the extent that we desire it, to the extent that we wish it, to the extent that we are worthy, divine grace comes through our brother."[3]

St. Porphyrios insists that joy is characteristic of those who have Christ in their hearts. He believes Christians should be "joyful" in their spiritual practices: "Fast as much as you can, make as many prostrations as you can, attend as many vigils as you like, but be joyful." Christians should strive not to practice the Church's different customs, traditions, and discipline but, most importantly, to "find a way to enter into the light of Christ" to allow the divine eros to touch their hearts and souls. This is, for him, a taste of Paradise: "What is Paradise? It is Christ. Paradise begins here and now. It is the same: those who experience Christ here on earth experience paradise."[4] For St. Porphyrios, "hell is separation from Christ, the absence of love. In this world, we have a choice either to be with Christ and live with the joy of his presence in us or live apart from Him and taste this life as hell."[5] Christians should strive to love Christ, their neighbor, and everyone, including their enemies. In his view, loving ourselves is realized by loving Christ and our neighbor. "That is Christianity: through love for our brother to arrive at love for God."[6]

St. Porphyrios recognizes the pervasiveness of sin and human weakness in the present world and urges Christians not to despair.

---

3   Ibid.
4   Ibid, p. 96.
5   Ibid. p. 97.
6   Ibid.

Christians must live with hope: "It is bad to despair because someone who despairs becomes embittered and loses his willingness and strength. Someone who has hope, on the contrary, advances forward." Amid the trials and tribulations that permeate life in the present world, Christians should unceasingly strive to advance and deepen their unity with Christ so they feel the joy of His presence in their lives. They should constantly explore ways to love Christ and be present in all their thoughts and actions. This intimate relationship with Christ gives them the grace to endure as they cope with life's challenges.

Falling in love with Christ liberates Christians from loneliness. Those who have fallen in love with Christ are "peaceable, joyous, full." They do not experience melancholy, illness, pressure, anxiety, depression, or hell. They endure injustices with joy. They can even suffer unjustly as Christ has unjustifiably suffered. If Christ has entered our hearts, we cannot swear, hate, seek revenge, or have other passions. He questions: How could there be in our hearts hatred, dislikes, censure, egotism, anxiety, and depression? The joy of Christ's presence liberates us from the passions that alienate us from our true nature, to be the visible presence of Christ in the world.

How does a Christian understand the inevitability of death, the physical separation of body and soul that all humans experience as mortal beings? St. Porphyrios confessed when he was seriously ill to the point of leaving this life, his mind was set primarily on Christ's love and inheritance of eternal life. This love made him think not about his sins but about the joy of meeting his beloved. It led him to believe that death is a bridge Christians will cross instantly to continue their life in Christ. Reflecting on the possibility of his imminent death, he confessed: "I didn't want to feel fear. I wanted to go to the Lord and think about His goodness. His love." St. Porphyrios desired to surrender wholeheartedly to Christ's love and be happy where he would send him. He confessed that when the time comes to stand in the presence of Christ for judgment, he will bow his head and say to Him: 'Whatever you want, my Lord, whatever your love desires. I know I am not worthy. Send me wherever your love wishes.

I am fit for hell. And place me in hell as long as I am with You. There is one thing I want, one thing I desire, one thing I ask for, and that is to be with You, wherever and however You wish."[7]

---

7   Ibid. p. 98.

XX

THE JOY OF BEING WITH CHRIST
IN HIS CHURCH

Saint Porphyrios, a Greek Orthodox monk who died in 1991, was formally glorified as a saint by the Ecumenical Patriarchate in November 2013. He stands in the long tradition of charismatic spiritual guides in the Orthodox Church. His book *Wounded by Love* narrates his life and teachings, expressing the richness of the ascetic, mystical Orthodox tradition. His theology reflects Orthodoxy's authentic, charismatic aspects, a fruit of prayer, ascesis, and love for God and others. St. Porphyrios, based on his ascetic and mystical experience of living with Christ in the Church, shares his understanding of how the faithful should understand their relationship with Christ in the Church and what that entails.

St. Porphyrios went to school for only one year, and while looking after the sheep as a young child, he read on his own, "syllable by syllable," the life of St John the Hut-dweller. As a result of this reading, St. Porphyrios wanted to become a monk. Later, when he went to Mount Athos, he was introduced to the spiritual and ascetical traditions of the Church by his elder, to whom he was obedient and learned to read by reading the lives of the saints, the Psalter, the Book of Eight Tones (the *Octoechos*) and the Menaia. In our judgment, St. Porphyrios exemplifies the authentic spirit of Orthodoxy, an essential reminder that the authenticity of Orthodox theology depends primarily on the Church's liturgical, hagiological, and ascetical tradition and practice. His writing aimed to inform the faithful about the significance of the Church, its origins, its identification with Christ, and how the faithful should understand and sustain their relationship with Christ within the Church.

For St. Porphyrios, the Church is rooted in God's trinitarian life and creative Love (Eph. 1.4). "The three persons of the Trinity constitute the eternal Church. *The Church is a divine institution and in her dwells the fullness of divinity.*"[1] God created humans in His image and likeness, aiming for humanity and Creation to live within the "eternal Church," the communion of three persons of the Trinity. He bestowed everything to humans so they become gods through grace. Yet, humans used their freedom poorly, lost their original beauty and righteousness, and cut themselves from God. Thus, they alienated themselves from God and lost Paradise. However, God, in his compassionate Love, did not abandon humanity and Creation in their estranged condition. The incarnation of His Logos opened the gates of Paradise and granted salvation to the world. Humanity entered "the eternal Church," the trinitarian communion through Christ. "On entering the uncreated Church, we come to Christ; we enter the realm of the uncreated." In the words of St. Porphyrios, the vocation of the faithful is "to become uncreated beings by grace, to become participants in the divine energies of God, to enter the mystery of divinity, to surpass their worldly frame of mind, to die to the "old man," and to become immersed in God."

The Church, after the incarnation, is the very presence of God in history that embraces humanity and the whole of Creation. Christ is the head of the Church, and the faithful are His body. The Church and Christ are one. "The body of the Church is nourished, sanctified, and lives in Christ. He is the Lord, omnipotent, omniscient, everywhere present and filling all things, our staff, our friend, our brother: the pillar and sure foundation of the Church." The Church for St. Porphyrios is a cosmic reality. In the Church, Christ unites all creation. "Christ united the body of the Church with heaven and

---

1 Wounded by Love, p. 87.

earth: with angels, men, and all created things, with all of God's creation – with animals and birds, with each tiny wildflower and microscopic insect. The Church became the fullness of Him who fills all in all, that is, of Christ. Everything is in Christ and with Christ. This is the mystery of the Church."

A faithful relationship with Christ in the Church is not simply a relationship of an individual with Him, independently of or apart from the rest of the faithful. St. Porphyrios insists that people's unity and love for Christ are revealed in the love that each of them has for one another: "On my own, I am not the Church, but together with you. Altogether, we are incorporated into Christ and become the Church." (I Cor 12.27) People's entrance into the Church unites them with their fellow men with their joys and sorrows; they feel the suffering and the affliction of others to be their own and pray for everyone to be saved. They do everything for their suffering brethren just as Christ did for them.

It is a mistake for someone to pray in the Church only for their salvation. "We must love others and pray that no soul be lost, that all may enter the church." St. Porphyrios insists: "When we set ourselves apart from others, we are not Christians. We are true Christians when we have a profound sense that we are members of the mystical body of Christ, of the Church, in an unbroken relationship of love." The oneness with Christ that we experience in the Church includes all people worldwide, regardless of the geographical space in which they find themselves. "However far away our fellow human beings may be, we must stand by them... when Christ unites us, distances don't exist." We pray to God to enlighten and change them so they may come to Christ. In their unity with Christ in the Church, the faithful embrace love, compassion, and prayers for all human beings, including those who are not "close to the Church, those who are distant to Christ.

To be Christian in the Church is to live with and in Christ. Life in Christ becomes humanly possible primarily through God's grace and personal efforts. This kind of life leads humanity into a different state of being, "another, enviable state" of existence. In that state of being, "there is no fear: neither of death or the Devil nor hell. All these things exist for people who are far from Christ, for non-Christians. For Christians who do God's will, as the Gospel says, these things do not exist." What St. Porphyrios here means is that by renouncing "the old self" with its passions and desires, one gives no importance to the Devil or evil. It does not concern those who are truly united with Christ. What concerns them is Love and service to Christ and their fellow man. If they feel joy, love, and worship of God without fear, they say, it is no longer I who lives; Christ lives in me (Gal. 2.20). We become authentic human beings loving Christ, the Church, and our neighbor. Christians must love, worship, and desire to be with God as they strive to be with Christ, their neighbor, and everyone, including their enemies. The Christian cares for everyone; he wants all to be saved and taste the Kingdom of God. *That is Christianity: through love for our brother to arrive at love for God...when we love our brother, we love the Church and Christ.* [2]

St. Porphyrios states that in the liturgical life of the Church, in worship, people experience here and now Paradise; they participate in God's trinitarian life. In his view, Paradise begins here and now. The different images that identify Paradise with gardens with flowers, mountains, streams, and birds are mediums for envisioning the beauty of Paradise. These images must not be taken literally since "Paradise is something else, something very exalted." He identifies Paradise with Christ, and those who experience Christ here on earth experience paradise. The Church is Paradise on earth, the same as Paradise in heaven. [3]

The experience of Paradise is accessible to the faithful through their participation in the sacramental life of the Church. In the sacraments and, above all, in the Holy Eucharist, "Christ offers Himself to the world." The sacraments express the Spirit of Orthodoxy, which is nothing else than unity with Christ. "The Church is the new life in Christ. In the Church, there is no death and no hell. Saint John the Evangelist says: Whoever keeps my word

---

2 *Wounded by Love*, p. 97.
3 *Wounded by Love*, p. 96.

will never taste death (John 8.52). Christ does away with death. Whoever enters the Church is saved; he becomes eternal. Life is one, an unbroken continuity: there is no end, no death. Whoever follows Christ's commandments never dies. He dies according to the flesh, according to passions, and, starting from this present life, is accorded to live in Paradise in our Church and, after that, in eternity. *"Death becomes the bridge we will cross with Christ instantly to continue living in the unsetting light."*[4] Thus, there is no despair in the Church. Asking the compassionate and loving God to forgive us, and through our participation in the Church's sacramental life, "we progress towards immortality, without anxiety and fear."

For St. Porphyrios, the Orthodox faith (our religion) originates in God's revelation. It is "the authentic and true religion." What differentiates the Orthodox from other faiths (beliefs) is that "other religions" do not know the greatness of the Triune God. They do not know that our destiny is to become gods according to grace, attain likeness with the Triune God, and become one with Him and among ourselves." Here, the work of Christ finds completion. St. Porphyrios recognized that for some, living the Orthodox faith is a struggle, a source of agony and anxiety for many. They do not experience "the deeper meaning of their faith." Their faith is reduced to "an illness, and indeed a terrible illness." They are "filled with agony and anxiety." They do prostrations and weep and practice their faith as coercion, forgetting that whatever is done under pressure always causes the soul to react with rejection. Such people experience their faith as a kind of hell. Despite their good intentions, it is not unusual for some of them not to receive God's grace through their labor, prostrations, and crossing. He attributes this failure to the fact that they are not humble and do not go beyond the formal aspects of the Church practices to the heart of the matter, which is to do everything with love. "Love attracts the grace of God. When grace comes, then the gifts of the Spirit come. The fruits of the Spirit are Love, joy, peace, long-suffering, gentleness, goodness, faith, meekness, and self-control. These are the things that a healthy soul in Christ should have."

---

4 Ibid. p. 99.

Christ is the joy that transforms those genuinely united with Christ in His Church. "Have Christ's joy. It is the joy that lasts forever, that brings eternal happiness. The joy of our Lord gives assured serenity, serene delight, the all-joyful joy that surpasses every joy." (John 16.24 & I John 1.4) *Christ desires to enrich us with joy. Most of all, this is what He wants to fill us with joy because He is the well-spring of joy.*

XXI
THE HOLY SPIRIT AND THE CHURCH

Through the power of the Holy Spirit, God raises Jesus Christ from the dead and incorporates believers into His resurrectional life: "You have been raised with him...in Christ Jesus" (Col. 2.12; cf. Eph. 2.5ff.). Thanks to the Spirit, the faithful become the body of Christ: "For by one Spirit we were all baptized into one body," which is "the body of Christ" (I Cor 12.13, 27). The presence of the Spirit in the faithful guides them into adherence to Christ: "Unless you possessed the Spirit of Christ, you would not belong to him" (Rom. 8.9ff.). The experience of the Spirit in the present is the beginning (ἀπαρχή) and advance pledge or foretaste (ἀρραβών) of the coming kingdom of glory (Rom. 8.23; II Cor. 1.22; Eph. 1.14). It is the experience of life's new beginning, the springtime of life, a new birth, and a new start. According to St. Paul, the Church is the body of Christ in glory; she is not an addition since she is His body, "brought to life with Christ" (cf. Eph. 2.5ff.).

Jesus Himself rose from the dead as a community: the Easter event is the coming of the Church. The Holy Spirit participates from the very beginning in the coming of the Church since it is in the Spirit that the Father raises Christ to life. At Pentecost, the risen and glorified Christ bestows the Holy Spirit upon those who believe in Him: "God raised Jesus to life.... Now raised to the heights by God's right hand, he has received from the Father the promise of the Holy Spirit... and what you see and hear is the outpouring of that Spirit" (Acts 2.32.). The Holy Spirit enabled the early Church to manifest her unity with God through the risen Christ.

The Holy Spirit's gifts enrich the Church's life and make her unity with Christ inclusive of diversity. The Holy Spirit endows the life of the Church with the gifts of speaking in tongues (Acts 2.4ff; 10.46; 19.6), praising God (Acts 10.46), bold proclamation (Acts 2.11; 4.8; 4.31), power in confrontation (Acts 6.10; 13.9), new Christian prophecy (Acts 2.17-18; 11.28; 20.23; 21.4; 21.11), vision (Acts 7.55), and guidance (Acts 8.29; 10.19; 11.12; 13.2).[1]

St. Paul describes the mystery of the Church by affirming that the faithful exist and live "in Christ" and "in the Spirit." The faithful are justified and sanctified "in Christ" and "in the Spirit" (cf. I Cor. 1.2, 30; II Cor. 5.21; Rom. 14.17; 15.16); they possess joy and peace in both (cf. Phil. 3.1; 4.7; Rom. 14.17); the love of God is obtained for them in Christ (cf. Rom. 8.39) and in the Spirit (cf. Col. 1.8). St. Paul states: "Christ is in you" (Rom. 8.10) and "the Spirit of God has made his home in you" (Rom. 8.9); in both Christ and the Spirit the faithful are sons of God (cf. Gal. 4.1-7). Here, St. Paul communicates the essential belief of the early Church of the unity between the Spirit and Christ. The Spirit of God's power is also the Spirit of Christ. Yet the Spirit of God and Christ, in distinct ways, communicate the will of God in bringing the coming reign of God to the world through the believers. The Spirit inhabits the believer of whom he makes a temple of God: "You are God's temple, and the Spirit of God is living among you" (cf. I Cor. 3.16). The Apostle never says that the Christian is the temple of Christ. Christ does not

---

1 The community experienced the Spirit in the courage through which it was able to preach Jesus in a hostile world. This is what their Lord had promised them in Acts 1.8. Peter even says that the apostles are witnesses of Jesus and the Holy Spirit (Acts 5.32). Likewise, we are told that Apollos was fervent in spirit when he preached Jesus (18.25). The community experienced the help of the Spirit not only in courts of law but also where it surrendered to his guidance in its preaching and tried to listen to God before setting off on its own. Thus, the Spirit showed the Church how to proceed in proclaiming the Gospel. Philip was sent to the Ethiopian treasurer (8.29); Peter, against his own wishes, to the Gentile Cornelius (10.19; 11.12); Paul and Barnabas on their first missionary journey (13.2,4).

inhabit the house; he is the foundation (cf. 1 Cor. 3.11; Eph. 2.20) and the entire building, of which the faithful form part; similarly, he is the head and the whole body, of which the faithful are the members. The faithful are the temple where the Spirit dwells, but they are the body of Christ where the Spirit reigns. The difference is indwelling and incorporation; the believer is incorporated into Christ and inhabited by the Spirit.

For the Spirit does not appropriate the faithful to himself; his action is at the service of the Son. In raising Christ to life, through dwelling in him and sanctifying him, he incorporates men into him so that they may rise again and be sanctified through him. However, Christ is not just a platform on which the Spirit is to build the Church. He has at his service the power of the Spirit (cf. Titus 3.6), and through it, he unites men into his body. How does he do this? Power is love; by giving himself to men, he unites them to himself. The Eucharist manifests this; here, he incorporates the congregation into himself. Thus, the Church depends in every respect on her double, indivisible origin.

The Church, according to St. Paul, is the new Covenant (cf. Gal. 4.24, 26), the one announced by Jeremiah (31.31) in which the heart of man is full of the Holy Spirit (cf. 36.27). It finds its expression in the celebration of the Holy Eucharist of which it is said: "This cup is the new covenant in my blood" (Lk. 22.20; I Cor. 11.25). Christ presides invisibly and all the faithful celebrate with him the paschal mystery. The Eucharist structures and shapes the life of the Church. "If there are distinctions in the Church's structures, they are not intended to separate but to unite. Thus, the difference that characterizes the priest does not separate him from the faithful; they do not confront each other, nor is he above them; he is drawn into the community, making his ministry central. The spirit of communion is the basis of the Church's structure. The spirit of communion tends to make everything in the Church personal; he imprints a personal stamp on the ecclesial covenant. The Church is not just a group of individuals; its members are bound to one another by personal bonds; the institution is a network of personal relationships. "The institutional aspect, inevitable in the Church on Earth, must ceaselessly be converted from bureaucracy to personal relationships. The personalization goes so far that the whole Church can be found, in reduced form, in each believer's person 'The whole Church is in each one.' The ecclesial institution is faithful to the Spirit who creates it in the measure it brings about a community of persons, in which the ministries are community creators.

One, Yet Made of Many Parts

The Church is one, for Christ, with whom she forms one body, is not divided. Unity thus looked at may seem to be uniformity, since in Christ, there are no more distinctions between Jew and Greek... male and female" (Gal. 3.28), and all are one in him. But it is in the Spirit that the Church is baptized into one Christ (cf. I Cor. 12.13); by this fact, the Apostle finds her one, yet made up of many parts, one in an abundance of diversity (cf. I Cor. 12.4-30). The Spirit's role is to unite while diversifying and manifesting each one's identity. He acts, in that He is love, by creating beings who form relationships, where the union of persons does not abolish but accentuates the identity of each in the interplaying of relationships. In the Church, there is unity in diversity, just as God is one in the Trinity.

The Spirit is paradoxical also in this respect; unique yet unifying – 'in one Spirit' (I Cor. 12.13) – He is lavish. The faithful constitute a single body in the diversity of the members; great is the variety of ministries and the gifts of the Spirit, which are all exercised in the body of Christ-given unity (cf. I Cor. 12.4-30).

What is the image of the temple? It reminds us of the idea of space that is lived in, but the Spirit transcends space; He cannot be contained by it. Local presence is not the only one known to man; there is another, personal, where the "I" of the one and that of the other come close to each other and, to a certain degree, are joined together and penetrate each other. This presence is the effect of a love that makes a reciprocal inwardness possible. "The one who loves comes out of himself and is transferred into the beloved." This is how the Father and the Son are present to each other: "I am in the Father and the Father is in me" (Jn. 14.10). A similar union takes place between Christ and the believer: You will understand that I am in my Father, and you in me and I in you" (Jn. 14.20).

However, the indwelling of the Spirit is different. The Spirit doesn't establish the reciprocal inwardness between Himself and the believer of two people united in friendship. He is love; He provokes the union, but He does not bring it about for His benefit: He works for the Father and the Son. He is present in the union between people and anointing, which impregnates the "I" and makes it capable of a relationship. His presence is creative in relationships; it enables Christ and Paul to be united to the point where Paul can say, "Christ who lives in me" (Gal. 2.20). His presence is, therefore, basic; it establishes reciprocity. The Spirit is a bond of union. The love which 'causes one to be in love.' Through the presence of the Spirit, the believer belongs to Christ (cf. Rom. 8.9) and enters the relationship of the Son with the Father. The Spirit is the intimacy between God and His creature, the divine touch that brings about union, and love at the root of Christian love (cf. Rom 5.5). He divinizes the believer and introduces Him to the Trinitarian movement.

The Spirit is the ecstasy of God and the power of indwelling attraction to God: by His presence, the Trinity is rooted in the creature, and the creature is integrated into God. The Spirit is at the beginning: the Spirit enables the believer to open himself to communion; the Spirit is at the end; the Spirit is the seal that concentrates union.

St. Paul considers the Spirit to be the builder of the Christian community (I Cor. 12-14). Against the exaggerated emphasis that some in Corinth placed upon ecstatic phenomena such as speaking in tongues, he insists that the Spirit gives many different gifts and that those that benefit an individual in isolation are less valuable than those that edify the Church. Incomprehensible utterances are of much less value than coherent prophecies, and above all, the highest gift is love, which strengthens the whole body.

The Church is one, for Christ, with whom she forms one body, is not divided. The oneness of the Church is sometimes conceived as exclusive of diversity since in Christ, "there are no more distinctions between Jew and Greek... male and female" (Gal. 3.28), and all are one in Him. But it is in the Spirit that the Church is baptized into the oneness of Christ (cf. I Cor. 12.13); by this fact, the oneness of the Church is inclusive of abundant diversity (cf. I Cor. 12.4-30). The Spirit's role is to unite while diversifying and manifesting each person's identity. He acts in that He is love by creating beings that form relationships, where the union of persons does not abolish but accentuates the identity of each in the interplay of relationships. In the Church, there is unity in diversity, just as God is one in the Trinity. The Spirit is paradoxical also in this respect: unique yet unifying – "in the one Spirit" (I Cor. 12.13). The faithful constitute a single body in the diversity of members; great is the variety of ministries and the gifts of the Spirit, which are all exercised in the body of Christ given its unity (cf. I Cor. 12.4-30). We might think that a Church that tends to uniformity risks atrophy or turmoil, for it might stifle the Spirit who brings about unity in diversity.

The Church is holy in Christ Jesus (cf. I Cor. 1.2; Phil. 1.1) and in the Spirit of our God (cf. I Cor. 6.11). The Church and each believer are a temple in which the Holy Spirit makes His dwelling place (cf. I Cor. 3.16; 6.19; Eph. 2.20, 22). Yet the Spirit, although He dwells in the Church and each believer, cannot be contained or limited by them. He transcends them to fill the whole creation with God's sustaining and transforming grace. The Spirit acts in the world as the presence of God, which affects the hearts of believers and constitutes the community of God's people in the risen Christ.

XXII
THE HOLY SPIRIT AND CREATION

All things are called to live through God's Spirit and His Word since Yahweh's *Ruach* as the breath of God's voice and His *dabar* (word) can only exist in unity with each other "By the word of the Lord the heavens were made, and all their host by the *Ruach* of His mouth" (Psalm 33.6). The belief in God as Creator of Heaven and Earth that Israel held remained an unquestionable reality for the Christian Church. This explains why, in the New Testament, creation and the creative role of the Holy Spirit are not mentioned explicitly. The participation of the Spirit together with the Word in God's creative act is also affirmed in the patristic tradition. St. Irenaeus stated that the Father has His Word, His Son, and His Wisdom, His Spirit; these are His "two hands" by which He created all things. St. Athanasius noted that "the Father creates all things through the Word in the Holy Spirit" and that "things created through the Word have their vital strength out of the Spirit from the Word." St. Basil further explains the Trinitarian action of God in creation in the following manner:

> When you consider creation, I advise you to first think of Him who is the first cause of everything that exists: namely, the Father, and then of the Son, who is the creator, and then the Holy Spirit, the perfector... The Originator of all things is One: He creates through the Son and perfects through the Spirit. The Father creates through His will alone and does not need the Son yet chooses

to work through the Son. Likewise, the Son works as the Father's likeness and requires no other cooperation, but He decides to have His work completed through the Spirit.[1]

The participation of the Spirit in God's creative act is the basis upon which the relationship of the Spirit to nature as well as to the moral, cultural, and political life of the world depends. Suppose the Spirit did not participate in God's creative act by which the universe came into being. In that case, the Spirit becomes too sacralized, too tied to holy objects and events, and thus, the life of the world apart from or independent of the Church appears void of God's presence. By affirming the active participation of the Spirit in God's creative and sustaining acts, we find God, through the Holy Spirit, to be actively present in the life of the whole universe, a presence that precedes the personal or particular operation of the Spirit through the prayer of the Church. This understanding overcomes the subjective, privatizing view of the Spirit characteristic of pietism while positively viewing the experiential dimension of pneumatology.

The Spirit of God in Scripture is active in nature itself. The Spirit of God caused the east wind (Exod. 14.21), which blew for a whole night at the right time to make the shallowest part of the Red Sea passable. Psalm 147.18 describes what occurs every spring when the thaw begins, and the snow melts: "He makes his wind [or spirit] blow and the waters flow." In the warm breezes of spring, the Israelites saw the presence and activity of God in His "spirit," which thaws the ice and snow (cf. Is. 27.8). Life in general, including human life, is animated by God's Spirit. Thus, Psalm 104.27-31 says of all living things:

These all look to thee to give them their food in due season...

When thou hidest thy face, they are dismayed;

When thou takest away their ruach, they die and return to their dust.

---

1 *On the Holy Spirit*, 16.38.

When thou sendest forth thy ruach, they are created;

and thou renewest the face of the ground.

Here, the Spirit of God is pictured in anthropomorphic terms. God exhales, and His breath puts life into His creatures. Because people perceived the essence of life to be in inhaling and exhaling, *ruach* was also the term used for the breath of life and the power to live enjoyed alike by human beings and animals (Eccl. 12.7; 3.21). Wherever life is awakened, it is the work of God's breath or Spirit. But where death occurs, it is His breath or Spirit that departs. Job 33.4 affirms that life is a gift of the Holy Spirit: "The *Ruach* of God has made me, and the breath of the Almighty gives me life."

God's creative power is communicated to the beings he has created so that when talking about *ruach*, we also talk about their life's energy. The *ruach* as Yahweh's *ruach* is transcendent in origin, but it is equally true to say that as the power of life in all things, it is immanently efficacious... When we think about the ruach, we have to say that God is in all things, and all things are in God – though this does not mean making God the same as everything else. Life, even in its purely biological aspect, is the effect of the creative Spirit of God: "Thus says the Lord, who stretched out the heavens and formed the spirit of man within him" (Zech. 12.1). Life is the Spirit's gift that needs to be adored and respected.

The Holy Spirit and the New Creation

In Scripture, the Holy Spirit is not simply identified with God's creative and sustaining presence in the world's life; its outpouring is always identified with the fulfillment of Israel's eschatological hopes. From the beginning, Israel's faith was oriented to promise and the future it contained. In Joel 2.28-32 the message of hope amid devastation is manifested in a universal charismatic outpouring of the Spirit touching Israel's present and future. Isaiah (32.15) and Ezekiel (11.19; 36.26-27) link the spirit to Israel's glory, not in the past but in the future.

The eschatological outpouring of *Ruach* was bound up with a broader hope for the renewal of the ravaged land, of the nation, and of its relation to God (Isa. 32.14-18; 44.3-5; Ezek. 36.24-28; cf. also 37.12-14). This is very much a corporate hope; the *Ruach* of God's presence is the power of the restored life of Israel, not merely the inspiration of individuals. The Spirit of God will change the wilderness into a paradise and make it a place of justice and righteousness, and He will instill a new heart in the people (Ezek. 11.9; 18.31; 36.27; cf. Ps. 51.12). In Ezekiel's vision of the valley of dry bones, the eschatological salvation is like a resurrection from the dead. God will raise His people from the dead by granting to them His Spirit (Ezek. 37.14). The Spirit will make the people God's people: "They shall be my people," gathered as one nation in their land under one king, and "I will be their God" (Ezek. 37.21-23). Such hopes, beyond the immediate historical significance in the life of Israel, shaped the longing for the anointed one:

> Behold my servant, whom I uphold,
> my chosen, in whom my soul delights;
> I have put my *ruach* upon him,
> He will bring justice to the nations.
> He will not cry or lift up his voice,
> or make it heard in the street;
> A bruised reed he will not break,
> and a dimly burning wick he will not quench;
> he will faithfully bring forth justice.
> He will not fail nor be discouraged
> till he has established justice in the earth;
> and the coastlands wait for his law (Isa 42.1-4).

The hope of Israel's restoration to friendship with God was naturally expressed in terms of a new outpouring of God's Spirit upon the nation (Joel 2.28-29):

> And it shall come to pass afterward,
> that I will pour out my *ruach* upon all flesh;
> your sons and your daughters shall prophesy,

your old men shall dream dreams,
and your young men shall see visions.
Even upon the menservants and maidservants
in those days, I will pour out my *ruach*.

In the prophetic tradition, it is abundantly clear that God and His Spirit are not bound to the world as humanity sees it or, even more, as humanity has made it. For the prophets, there is a world beyond humanity's reach where the Holy Spirit reigns. This world is the future of our world after God and His justice and peace have judged it and have abolished the evil and the injustice of humanity. This prophetic hope for God's ultimate triumph assigns an eschatological function to the Spirit.

The active presence of the Holy Spirit in the world among the covenant people is a pledge of a new, worldwide reality to come forth when God will overturn the kingdoms of this world, "not by might nor by power, but by my Spirit, says the Lord" (Zech. 4.6; cf. 6.1-8) and establish His everlasting Kingdom. To the disillusioned people, the Lord said through the Prophet Haggai: "Take courage...I am with you, says the Lord...My Spirit abides among you; fear not" (2.4-5). God assures His people who live under oppressive and discouraging conditions that His Spirit and Word shall be with them (Is. 59.21; cf. 9.20,30). The presence and experience of God, which is expected from the coming of the Spirit:

Universal – no longer particular, but related to 'all flesh' in the whole breadth of creation;

Total – no longer partial, effective in the human 'heart,' in the depths of human existence.

Enduring – no longer historical or temporary, but conceived as the 'resting' or 'dwelling' of the Spirit;

Direct – no longer mediated through revelation and tradition but grounded on contemplating God and his glory.

The Christian Church believes that what the prophets had expected to come at the end has already been fulfilled in Jesus Christ and the descent of the Spirit upon his disciples. The Spirit has already been given to all who believe in Jesus Christ as Lord and Savior. What happened at Pentecost when the Spirit came among the little group of Jesus' disciples was, for St. Luke, a sign that the "last days" have broken in. St. Paul suggested that the new creation begins wherever a man lives "in Christ" (II Cor. 5.17). Creation, when God caused light to shine out of darkness, repeats itself whenever a person is allowed to see the glory of God in the face of Christ through the proclamation granted by the Holy Spirit (II Cor. 4.6). St. John and the author of the Epistle to Titus suggest that new birth or regeneration occurs in baptism, when a person through the power of the Holy Spirit begins to open to Jesus Christ (Jn. 3.3-7; Titus 3.5).

Although we experience God's glory through the power and enlightenment of the Holy Spirit, we and our spirit-filled communities continue to live in history, and our lives are affected by all the fragmentation, evil, and corruption in this world. We experience sacramentally the presence of God, but we do not yet live in heaven. The new creation is present in history but is not yet history. This new creation will be finally realized only when God does away with all our afflictions, suffering, and death. This point is made in II Corinthians 1.22 and 5.5 and Ephesians 1.13-14 with the term "guarantee." The Spirit is, as it were, a down payment. He is the "Spirit of promise" of greater gifts in the future (Eph. 1.13). He enkindles something of God's new world even in this world, or as Hebrews 6.4-5 puts it, He allows us to taste the power of God's future. This gift of the Spirit is a 'pledge' (ἀρραβών) (II Cor. 1.22; 5.50), a "first fruit" or "down payment" (ἀπαρχή) (Rom. 8.23) of what God is offering to His beloved creation. It points beyond the resurrection to "the redemption of our bodies" (Rom. 8.23) when the whole creation "will be set free from its bondage to decay and obtain the glorious liberty of the sons of God" (Rom. 8.21). This eschatological dynamic is fundamental to the work of the Spirit. It is the power of God driving toward the end of history and carrying us forward to the destiny disclosed and anticipated in the resurrection of Jesus Christ.

The new creation by the Spirit is not a flight by faith into heaven but rather a recognition of the world's limitations and a commitment to bring the freedom that the Holy Spirit grants from death, corruption, and evil to the world. The eschatological future in the Christian tradition is strongly determined by the negation of the negative and openness to the development of the positive. The negation of the negative is described in Revelation 21.4: "God will wipe away every tear from their eyes, and death shall be no more, neither shall there be mourning nor crying nor pain anymore." The further development of the favorable condition is reflected: "They shall be his people, and he himself, God with them, shall be their God.... And he who sat upon the throne said, 'Behold, I make all things new'" (Rev. 21.3, 5). God has given to the world, through His Church, the Holy Spirit as a foretaste and promise of all that is yet to come

XXIII

THE NATURE AND
THE MISSION OF THE CHURCH

The Nicene-Constantinopolitan Creed expresses the faith of the baptized faithful in one holy, catholic, and apostolic church. In the context of the creedal affirmations, the nature of the Church is understood in connection with and as a consequence of the work of the Holy Spirit. The life and mission of the Church in the world are primarily defined by God's gracious revelation and presence in the world through the Incarnate Word and the Holy Spirit. St. Irenaeus, in the second half of the second century, expressed this dependence:

> God's gifts are given to the Church, just as God breathed life into those he had fashioned out of earth so that all the members receive life in this way. And in this gift is the gift of Christ, that is, the Holy Spirit, contained – the promise of eternal life, the confirmation of our faith, and the way to God. God placed apostles, prophets, and teachers in the Church (I Cor. 12.28) and the general working of the Spirit. Those who depart from the Church lose their participation in this working of the Spirit... For where the Church is, there is also the Spirit of God. And where the Spirit of God is, there is also the Church and all grace, for the Spirit is the Truth.

Images of the Church in the New Testament

The Church, as the living community of the baptized disciples of Christ, has not been an object of systematic reflection in the Christian tradition. Christians began to reflect systematically on the nature and mission of the Church at the dawn of the ecumenical movement in their concerted efforts to overcome their divisions. Yet, ample theological resources exist in Scripture and the patristic literature about aspects of the Church's life and mission.

In the New Testament, the community of Christ's disciples is called the Ecclesia of God. Generally, Ecclesia stands for a people's assembly, a gathering of all people in a particular city. In the book of Acts, Ecclesia designates the Christian community of a specific place, whether it is in Jerusalem (5.11; 8.1, 3; 15.4, 22), in Antioch (11.26; 13.1; 14.27; 15.3) or places of the Pauline mission (e.g., Ephesus). Because the term ecclesia designates a particular community located in a specific place, one speaks of "churches" in the plural when one wants to refer to several local communities (Rom. 16.4; 1 Cor. 16.19; 14.33f; 16.1, 19, etc.). In some instances, the entirety of the Christian community is referred to as the Church. St. Paul described the persecution of Christians by him before his conversion as the persecution of the Church of God; in the Church of God, God has called up apostles, prophets, etc. (I Cor. 12.28). Ecclesia describes the coming together of the faithful to worship God through the memory of Jesus Christ (1 Cor. 11.18; cf. Also 1 Cor. 14. 34).

In the New Testament, the Church is portrayed through multiple images, but none of them, independently of the others, can communicate the fullness of the Church's nature and mission. In Christian tradition, the significant images by which the Church is referred to are the people of God, the body of Christ, and the temple of the Holy Spirit. The importance that one gives to one of these images over the others depends on their particular ecclesiological tradition and ethos.

The Church as the People of God

The designation and understanding of the Church as the people of God situates the Church in the context of Israel's eschatological expectations. According to the Hebrew way of thinking, the people form a whole, a corporate personality. As such, they take part in the events of history so that the individual is involved in the destiny of the whole, even in a supratemporal way. Israel, however, became the people of God because Yahweh chose it to be His possession (cf. Exod. 19.5; 23.22; Deut. 7.6; 14.2; 26.18). The whole faith of Judaism can be summed up in a single phrase: "I will take you as my people, and I will be your God." (Exod. 6.6- 8; 19.5f; Lev. 26.9; 11-12). As Israel, in its historical existence, was failing to live up to God's expectations, the prophets announced God's determination to re-establish His relationship with His people in a new, definitive, and indissoluble way: "They will be my people, and I will be their God... I will make an everlasting covenant with them and not cease to follow them to do them good." (Jer. 32.38ff.). Out of this fundamental prophetic promise, the belief was born that only the Israel of the eschatological future would indeed be the people of God.

The early Church, believing in Jesus Christ and receiving the Spirit of God at Pentecost, understood itself to be the eschatological people of God. In the First Epistle of Peter (2.9f.), the Church is referred to as a "chosen race," a "royal priesthood," a "holy nation," and "God's people," Such expressive predicates described in the Old Testament, the people of Israel and now tell what the Church is and has become. The words are spoken to the Church now: "I will live in them and move among them, and I will be their God, and they shall be my people."

The new people of God come to be because of God's freely given love and grace. They are a people because God dwells within them and moves among them (I Peter 2.9-10; Rom. 9.25-26). God has acquired them by the redeeming blood of His Son (Acts 20.28). Jesus Christ "has given Himself for us to redeem us from all iniquity and cleanse for Himself a people of His own" (Titus 2.14). The distinctiveness of the early Christian communities is asserted by the formula "in Christ" (Gal.1.22; I Thess. 2.14) that describes the newness of the Christian reality established by God. Thus, the understanding of the Church as the people of God provides us with a concept, which defines the continuity of the Church with Israel within God's plan of salvation.

This continuity of the Church with Israel within God's salvific plan defines the Church since its beginnings. A striking example of their persistence in this belief is the fact that they left Galilee after Jesus' resurrection, even though the first Easter appearances took place there. They assembled in Jerusalem and remained in the capital. The reason for this action was their belief that they stood in the midst of the last things, and they awaited the definitive revelation of the reign of God in Jerusalem, where, according to Jewish belief, the last events would run their course. In the context of this anticipation, the circle of the Twelve was reconstituted after the departing of Judas Iscariot by the election of a new member (cf. Acts 1.15-26). Another phenomenon that throws light on the self-understanding of the early Church is the practice of baptism (of Acts 2.38-42). Baptism was considered to be an eschatological act for Israel; the people of God were to be sealed in preparation for the coming end, for the purpose to be ready to endure the judgment of the Son of Man.

The Church as the Body of Christ

The notion of the Church as the Body of Christ in the writings of St. Paul is a helpful image by which the unity of the believers with Christ is affirmed. It refers to the ontological reality of Christ's presence in the world as a community (I Cor. 12.12b; 12.27; 6.15). In I Corinthians 6.15-17 the members of the Church as members of Christ are ontologically identified through the Spirit with Christ's exalted body. This unity is disclosed most vividly in the celebration of the Eucharist through which the unity of the congregation as the "body of Christ" becomes physically manifested by their sharing in the one Eucharistic bread (I Cor. 10.17). Thus, what the Church already is through baptism (Gal. 3.26-28) is fully revealed in the Eucharist. The Church is a single body, the Body of Christ: "through baptism Christians join the one body (1 Cor. 12.13); through the sharing in the bread of the Lord's Supper, this unity is actualized and rendered concrete (1 Cor. 10.17)." In the accounts of Paul's conversion we also see that the Church that Paul was trying to stamp out was not other than Jesus Christ Himself: "Saul, Saul, why do you persecute me? ...And I said who are you, Lord? And the Lord said, 'I am Jesus whom you persecute'" (Acts 26.14f; cf. 9.4f; 22.7f). Thus, the Christian community can be conceived as a corporate personality whose identity and life is drawn from its ontological identification with Christ. However, although we can affirm that the resurrected body of Christ is the Christian community, we cannot also affirm that the Christian community is always the resurrected body of Christ. This is evident from the problem and the failures of the Church of Corinth. St. Paul reminds the Corinthians what they have become through God's gracious love and dispensation and invites them to live the newness of life by conforming to God's will and visibly manifest their oneness in Jesus Christ.

The Church is God's people constituted in Christ and in relation to Christ and the presence in them of God's Spirit. This is apparent in the Epistle to the Galatians, which describes the change from the period of the Law to that of grace (3.23-25) and refers to baptism as the act by which all "in Christ Jesus" have become sons of God, by "putting on Christ" (3.26f.). Because of this relationship, the Church, the community of the redeemed, emerges in which "there is neither Jew nor Greek, neither slave nor free, neither male nor female; for you are all one in Christ Jesus" (3.28).

XXIV

THE ORTHODOX CHURCH AND THE OTHER CHRISTIAN CHURCHES

The Orthodox Church maintains cordial relations with other Christian Churches and participates in joint efforts to recover the visible unity of all Christians. This effort precedes those aspects of faith that bring all Christian Churches and communions closer without ignoring the substantive doctrinal and theological differences that caused their separation. While most of the faithful perceive the involvement of the Orthodox Church in this joint quest for unity to be guided by the Holy Spirit, others express fear that the faith of the Church is somehow compromised for the sake of unity, not always grounded in truth. In this short article, we will try to address these concerns by responding to two critical questions: Why have the Orthodox Churches decided to be involved in the ecumenical movement for the unity of God's Church, and how does this involvement relate to their claim to be the embodiment of the one, holy, catholic and apostolic Church?

The Ecumenical Patriarchate, in an encyclical, addressed to all Orthodox Churches in 1902, invited the Orthodox Churches to move towards more dynamic inner communion, conciliarity, and cooperation to work with other Christian Churches and communities toward the visible unity of all Christians. This is the desire of our Lord Jesus Christ (John 17) and the prayer of the Church in her liturgy. This unity is presented in the encyclical as a gift of God's Spirit whose reception requires the sincere efforts of all who believe in Christ and "walk in the paths of the evangelical love and peace." In 1920, the Ecumenical Patriarchate issued a second encyclical addressed to all Christian Churches, suggesting the formation of a "league of churches" for common witness and action. It envisioned that the Churches could move towards greater unity if they could overcome their mutual mistrust and bitterness by rekindling and strengthening the evangelical love. This could lead them to see one another not as strangers and foreigners but as being part of the household of Christ and "fellow heirs, members of the same body and partakers of the promise of God in Christ" (Eph. 3.6). Such unity couldn't be advanced simply by just overcoming doctrinal differences. Still, it demands interchurch *diakonia* and common witness to God's love for the world's life. In 1986, the Third Preconciliar Pan-Orthodox conference unequivocally stated that the "Orthodox participation in the ecumenical movement does not run counter to the nature and history of the Orthodox Church. On the contrary, it constitutes the consistent expression of the apostolic faith within new historical conditions."

The Orthodox Churches understand their participation in the ecumenical movement as being inspired and guided by the Spirit of God, who wills all to be united with the risen Christ. Thus, it is not simply a response to God's reconciling love but a movement of the Holy Spirit in which the churches participate. The Spirit of God invites all to break down the walls of hostility, overcome isolation and self-sufficiency, and become a communion of love for God's glory. The Greek Orthodox theologian Nikos Nissiotis, in his opening address as Moderator of the Faith and Order Commission of the WCC in Bangalore (1978), stated that the churches transcend their confessional boundaries and heal their divisions when they let the Spirit of God guide their lives. "The Spirit is the advocate of the dynamic over the static, of the multiform over the uniform, of the exceptional over the regular, of the paradox over the normal." When the separated Churches gathered, affirming faith in Christ and searching for ways to actualize and experience their unity in God's eschatological promise, reflect in their fellowship and efforts towards unity the presence and operation of God's Spirit. "The operation of the Spirit fills the gaps, unites the oppositions, bridges the distances, links the different gifts of grace."

The endorsement of the ecumenical involvement does not necessarily mean that the Orthodox Churches have abandoned their ecclesiological claims; on the contrary, they participate in the ecumenical movement without compromising its essential faith to be the fullness of the one, holy, catholic, and apostolic Church. What facilitated the fuller participation of the Orthodox Churches in the ecumenical movement is the statement on "The Church, the Churches, and the World Council of Churches," produced in 1950 in Toronto by the World Council of Churches. The "Toronto Statement," as it came to be called, assured the Churches that their participation in the World Council of Churches in no way prejudices the outcome of the ongoing quest for unity, and neither would the Churches be obliged to change their ecclesiology. Although the World Council of Churches is understood as a "fellowship of Churches," the Toronto statement noted that "the member churches of the World Council consider the relationship of other churches to the holy catholic Church which the Creed professes as a subject for mutual consideration. Nevertheless, membership does not imply that each Church must regard the other member Churches as 'Churches' in the true and full sense of the word." It also recognized that member Churches retain the "constitutional right to ratify or to reject utterances or actions of the Council." The Toronto Statement facilitated the involvement of the Orthodox Churches in the ecumenical movement without compromising their understanding of the nature, mission, and witness of the Church.

While the Orthodox Churches may view involvement in the ecumenical movement as consistent with their ecclesiology, they have been unwilling to address the claims of other Christian Churches and communions concerning their relation/identity with the one, holy, catholic, and apostolic Church. This has immediate consequences in the ecumenical witness of the Orthodox Churches and makes ecumenism a divisive issue within the Orthodox Church. "We Orthodox," Metropolitan Kallistos Ware notes, "do not at the moment have an agreed attitude towards non-Orthodox Christians." Among the Orthodox Churches, different visions of ecumenism and inter-Christian reconciliations lead to conflicts about ecumenism. "Some of us [Orthodox] see ecumenism as a sign of hope, others as a pan-heresy. Some of us think Roman Catholics have true priesthood; others consider that they should be re-baptized. When we meet other Christians, we speak with a divided voice. Consequently, our participation in the ecumenical movement has been far less effective than it could and should have been."

Any attempt to address this problem theologically requires that we take the faith and the sensitivities of the Orthodox Church about the unity of the Church seriously. The Orthodox Church is especially sensitive to maintaining its continuity with the apostolic Church's faith, life, and witness. Every division in the history of the Church has been viewed as a denial of its nature, separation from Christ's body, and a departure from the temple of the Holy Spirit. The Church, coping with schism and apostasies, emphasized the importance of unity and promulgated canons to fortify its unity and communicate its belief that those who separate themselves from the *una Sancta* depart from the domain of God's salvific grace, *extra ecclesia nulla Salus* (outside the Church there is no salvation). While the Orthodox Church never refuted this belief, it refused to accept its practical consequences. Metropolitan John Zizioulas believes the problem of the limits of the Church and of the implication for those individuals and communities who exist outside of these limits continues to be an unresolved issue for Orthodox theology. He states: "it is certainly not easy to exclude from the realm and the operation of the Spirit so many Christians who do not belong to the Orthodox Church." He believes that baptism creates the limits of the Church and that "within this baptismal limit it is conceivable that there may be division, but any division within these limits is not the same as the division between the Church and those outside the baptismal limit." From this perspective, without baptism, there is no Church; within baptism, even if divisions exist, one may still speak of the Church.

The Orthodox Churches seem to have adopted an ecclesiological agnosticism that avoids reflection on the ecclesiological claims of other Christian Churches concerning their relation to the one, holy, catholic, and apostolic Church. Fr. Georges Florovsky has challenged this ecclesiological agnosticism. He has consistently argued that the Orthodox Churches make implicit judgments about the ecclesial nature of the other Christian Churches by admitting their members to the Orthodox Church either through re-baptism, Chrismation, or mere recital of the Creed. The Orthodox Churches, he maintains, need to rethink their understanding of schism about *una Sancta.*

Florovsky observes that in the history of the Church, there are occasions when the Church, by her very actions, gives one to understand that the sacraments of sectarians – and even of heretics – are valid, that the sacraments can be celebrated outside the strict canonical limits of the Church. The Church customarily receives adherents from sects – and even from heresies – not by way of baptism, thereby obviously meaning or supposing that they have already been baptized in their sects and heresies. In many cases, the Church receives adherents without chrism and sometimes clergy in their existing orders. Fr. Florovsky interprets the practices of the Church as a sign that, in the Orthodox tradition, the "mystical territory" of the Church extends beyond "her canonical borders." He argues that the Church as "a mystical organism" and "the sacramental body of Christ" couldn't be adequately described exclusively using canonical terms and categories. He also suggests that neither the recognition of sacramental grace outside of the boundaries of the Orthodox Church can be grounded in the notion of *economia,* which, in his view, entered the life of the Orthodox churches during a time of theological confusion and decadence.

The belief of St. Cyprian that there is no salvation outside of the canonical boundaries of the Church must be respected as a strong urge to maintain and respect the unity of God's Church. However, today's needs require it to be supplanted with the theology of schism advanced by St. Augustine. For St. Augustine, despite their formal separation from the *una Sancta,* schismatic and heretical communities maintain bonds of unity with it. All the separated

Christian churches are related to each other and in communion, however imperfectly, with the one, holy, catholic, and apostolic Church. Recognizing this relationality is warranted because many still unbroken bonds whereby the schismatic communities are held in unity with the One Church. These bonds, in the words of Florovsky, include "right belief, sincere devotion, the Word of God, and above all the grace of God, whichever heals the weak and supplies what is lacking." Thus, in every schismatic and heretical community, there is something of God that connects them with the life of God's Church. "What is valid in the sects is that which is in them from the Church, that which remains with them as their portion of the sacred inner core of the Church, that through which they are with the Church."

What does this mean for the participation of the Orthodox Churches in the ecumenical movement? The recognition of the operation of God's Spirit in other Christian Churches leads us to the acknowledgement that these Churches, in their ecumenical commitment, have the potential to enhance the life and the witness of the one, holy, catholic, and apostolic Church through the gifts that the Spirit of God has bestowed to these communities. The Churches recognize their limitation in their separation from one another and the need to move towards unity in faith, life, and witness, they need to receive with humility and appreciation the gifts God's Spirit has bestowed on each one of them.

The refusal of the Orthodox Churches to be in sacramental communion with other Christian Churches, despite the affirmation that they are imperfectly and incompletely members of the One Church of God, should not be perceived as a sign of arrogance; neither should it be a source of Orthodox triumphalism or self-sufficiency. On the contrary, it is a painful reminder that the unity of God's Church requires the fullness of the Apostolic faith and tradition. It does not allow the Churches to become complacent with relative unity and collaboration. This leads to an irrevocable and unabated commitment of the Orthodox Churches to the fellowship of Christian churches that seek jointly to discover their unity in faith, life, and witness.

XXV

THE POSTMODERN
CRITIQUE OF DIALOGUE

Postmodern thinkers challenge the notion that dialogue can bridge the gap between individuals with diverse worldviews and interests, thereby promoting a harmonious life characterized by justice and peace. Their skepticism arises from a profound distrust of universal truths and a tendency to favor specific perspectives in a pluralistic world.

Traditional dialogues often overlook the deep-seated disparities among participants, failing to acknowledge the historical and cultural baggage that each voice carries. This oversight can inadvertently perpetuate hierarchies, allowing dominant narratives to overshadow those that are marginalized. Postmodernists argue that the premise of dialogue to bridge differences can lead to the domination of certain groups by others.

To address this critique, postmodern thinkers emphasize the need to approach dialogue with heightened awareness of power dynamics and the ideological conditioning that shapes every interaction. They believe that public discourse should allow diverse voices, perspectives, and opinions without the pressure to reconcile them into a consistent account. Attempts to do so, they argue, will almost always result in the domination of some groups by others. In their view, dialogical knowledge does not necessarily lead to consensus or agreement regarding the essential aspects of public life and moral attitudes in a plural society. Instead, it highlights the importance of recognizing and addressing the power dynamics that influence their interactions.

Postmodernism emphasizes differences, arguing that various voices, perspectives, and opinions should be expressed without reconciliation or a consistent account. It asserts that dialogue across differences is impossible because understanding among people with differences is not feasible, and discourses across differences inevitably lead to the imposition of values and beliefs on others. Postmodernists also point out that dialogue often lacks sensitivity to the diverse conditions that exist among groups and overlooks the serious conflicts and historical instances of oppression that groups have experienced. In societies with unjust relations between people in different groups, such as races, genders, cultures, and religions, dialogue is unattainable.

Postmodern philosophers' critiques have influenced our understanding of what dialogue can and cannot achieve. Those who embrace postmodernism in religious studies remind us that everything we perceive, experience, and know is embedded in and shaped by our cultural and religious contexts. These critiques have profound implications for how dialogue is structured and understood in pluralistic societies. They challenge the assumption that dialogue inherently leads to mutual understanding and cooperation. Instead, postmodernists advocate for re-examining the foundations of dialogue, proposing frameworks that acknowledge and accommodate the complexities of human interaction without attempting to reduce them to simplistic agreements. This approach necessitates a shift in perspective – a move away from viewing dialogue as a means to achieve consensus and towards understanding it as a process of engaging with diversity in its fullest sense. In practice, this involves actively listening to all participants, especially those who have historically been marginalized or silenced. It requires acknowledging the power dynamics at play and creating spaces where these dynamics are minimized. The focus is not on erasing differences or finding common ground but on fostering an environment where differences can coexist and be explored without fear of domination or erasure.

This reimagined form of dialogue opens new possibilities for understanding and collaboration in an increasingly interconnected yet deeply divided world. It invites participants to approach dialogue not as a battleground for competing truths, but as a fertile ground for mutual discovery and respect. This perspective transforms dialogue into a tool for celebrating human diversity while addressing its challenges.

They also remind us that our historical and cultural settings are ideologically and politically conditioned. Instead of opting for universal truths, they have chosen a diversity of truths. This stance reflects their philosophical view that all truth claims are socially constructed and therefore particular. It also expresses their ethical concern to defend the right to hold and advocate for specific worldviews in the onslaught of imperialistic universal worldviews.

Interfaith dialogue is often criticized for assuming that some common ground or shared experience sustains it. However, religious beliefs are uncertain about the existence of such a "common something" as each perceives it differently. Without a common ground or knowledge of shared beliefs, different religions' beliefs and truth claims become incommensurable, making it impossible to grasp and assess one in light of the other. In postmodern jargon, this means that there is only one way to understand and evaluate another religion, and that is through your own religion. Since it is the sole way to engage with other traditions, you will naturally regard your religion as the best approach to evaluating the value of other traditions. Therefore, unless a religious believer wants to abandon her own religion and culture and migrate to another, she is challenged to remain fully committed to the religion in which she exists.

How does this particularist view envision the relationship between faith communities with different worldviews in our present-day society of porous boundaries and multireligious neighborhoods? Essentially, it proposes a kind of "good neighbor policy" among religions. Followers of differing religions should be kind to one another, respect each other, and allow each religion to remain in its own backyard. Yes, there will be occasions, perhaps necessities, when common problems arise in the neighborhood, but these will be *ad hoc* conversations and collaborations. Meet in some common space, do what you can, but then allow everyone to return to their own house and backyard.

This postmodern critique against dialogue that assumes differences has been criticized for its exaggerated view. However, dialogue across differences doesn't necessarily mean eliminating those differences or imposing one group's views on others. Instead, it can lead to understanding, cooperation, and accommodation, allowing for the coexistence of diverse perspectives within a broader framework of tolerance and respect. Differences among communities and individuals are inherent elements of sameness. Dialogue, or communication, enables them to bring their beliefs and practices to public exploration and validation. By accepting differences, we recognize the social reality of a plural world, reducing the potential for violent conflict and oppressive activity.

The critique of postmodernism emphasizes the need to reframe dialogue as a celebration of coexistence within diversity, rather than a pursuit of uniformity. This perspective suggests that dialogue can function as a space where differences are acknowledged and cherished as essential components of a pluralistic society.

In this context, dialogue becomes a dynamic process – a shared journey where participants engage with empathy and curiosity, rather than judgment. This reimagined form of dialogue fosters an environment where individuals and communities can articulate their unique perspectives while remaining open to the richness of unfamiliar narratives. It challenges participants to view dialogue as an opportunity to enrich their understanding of the human condition and the diverse expressions of faith, culture, and identity that characterize the world.

This contrasting perspective highlights the necessity of a nuanced approach to dialogue in pluralistic societies. Rather than striving for an unattainable universal consensus, dialogue can embrace the richness of diversity while promoting mutual respect and shared understanding. The fundamental premise here is not to eliminate differences, but to create spaces where constructive engagement can occur without overshadowing the unique identities and experiences of the participants. For interfaith dialogue, this involves acknowledging the incommensurability of beliefs while exploring opportunities for collaboration on pressing global issues such as climate change, social justice, and humanitarian crises. These collaborations could serve as practical platforms where faith traditions contribute their insights and resources to tackle shared challenges, respecting their distinct worldviews while working towards common goals.

Furthermore, dialogical frameworks could benefit from incorporating historical contexts and addressing past injustices. By doing so, they can become more inclusive and sensitive to the realities of marginalized groups, preventing dialogue from becoming a tool of dominance. This approach calls for redefining dialogue – not to dissolve differences but as a practice that honors plurality while fostering equitable partnerships and coexistence. In such societies, people may jointly seek ways to affirm the existing cultural diversity and regulate its dynamics by affirming those principles and practices that advance human dignity, rights, equality, freedom, justice, and equality for all.

XXVI

INTER-CHRISTIAN MARRIAGE

Marriage between Orthodox Christians with other Christians are a significant single source of converts to Orthodoxy and the most important source of disidentification from the Orthodox Church. While the impact of such marriages upon the Greek Orthodox Church in America has not been sociologically adequately monitored, analyzed, and studied, it is an increasing concern of the whole Church as it gropes to understand and respond to the challenges that she is facing. It is a challenge and a problem that needs to be understood in all its complexity before we can efficiently plan a pastoral response to it. Such an understanding will provide us with realistic expectations of what can be done and how successful we can be in coping with such a serious, complex and multifaceted phenomenon that conditions the present and future life of our Church.

The urgency of this pastoral issue is unraveled by estimates that in Roman Catholicism approximately fifty percent of those who marry non-Catholics eventually stop practicing their faith. Andrew Greeley in his book "Crisis in the Church" states that the phenomenon of disidentification is five times as high in mixed marriages as it is in those where both partners are Catholic. According to a major study sponsored by the Council of Jewish Federation, fifty-two percent of Jewish men and women who have married since 1985 took 'gentiles' for spouses. This is significant since in 1964 only nine percent were interfaith marriages. More significantly, the same study found three of every four children of these intermarriages are being raised Christians or with no religion at all. This trend, combined with a below replacement birth rate, a rising tide of divorce and virtual end to immigration, is shrinking the Jewish community. Do we have enough reasons or indications to conclude that the Greek-American community is not plagued by the same trends? Quite the contrary, it is my strong belief that we share the same problems with the Roman Catholic, the Jewish, and other religious communities in this country.

For the sake of clarity, we must define the appropriate term by which we can describe this serious pastoral issue that our Church encounters. The marriage between two baptized Christians cannot be called inter-Church since this would imply that we loosely accept the ecclesial nature of every Christian community that practices trinitarian baptism. It is preferable for Orthodoxy to call such marriages Inter-Christian or Ecumenical marriages. Such marriages are contrasted with marriages between Christian and non-Christian (inter-faith), and with marriages in which only one participant has active membership in a Christian church (mixed).

Inter-Christian marriages are a common phenomenon that affects all Christian churches living in pluralistic societies. Given the educational, economic, and social mobility of the people in the United States, it is entirely predictable that men and women of different faiths will meet, fall in love and marry in greater numbers than ever before. Consequently, intermarriage as the product of underlying strong social forces cannot be easily reversed by institutions or church hierarchy. This, however, does not mean that the religious outcome of such a marriage is somehow automatic. On the contrary, the religious outcome depends on the experiences of the couple and their relationship with their relatives.

Sociologists have uncovered numerous facts about patterns of inter-Christian marriage. Their findings can be summarized in four questions: 1. What are the trends and patterns in inter-faith marriage? 2. Who intermarries? 3. What happens to the religious faith and commitment of the intermarried? 4. Is inter-faith marriage less stable than single-faith marriage? These findings trace relative patterns that describe the dynamics of inter-Christian marriages.

What are the Trends and Patterns in Inter-Christian marriage?

The percentage of Greek Orthodox marrying other Christians has been inching upward for decades, and it will probably continue to increase. A strong predictor of the number of intermarriages is the percentage of Orthodox Christians in a State or region. The fewer eligible Orthodox marriage partners in the area, the more intermarriage occurs. Another strong predictor of intermarriage rates is whether ethnic or social class barriers exist in the locality and the impending mixing of young people across religious lines. Where the barriers exist, intermarriage rates are low. Finally, the number of opportunities that young single Greek Orthodox men and women have – or take advantage of – to meet and interact with one another significantly impacts the rates of intermarriage.

Why are inter-Christian marriages increasing? If the absence of ethnic or socioeconomic barriers produces higher intermarriage rates, one would expect that the gradual trends of weakening ethnic barriers in American society would produce more intermarriage. Urban youth, who formerly seldom ventured outside their Italian, German, Anglo-Saxon, or Greek neighborhoods, today are less conscious of their ethnic differences. In addition, they probably live in ethnically diverse suburbs. They are now in close contact with youth of all religions and ethnicities.

In a nationwide study of college students, Albert Gordon concluded that increasing college attendance is one source of higher rates of interfaith marriage. "Young people of varying backgrounds who attend college together have this education and environment in common and are less likely to concern themselves with differences in family background, origin, or religion." In our society, much freedom is given to young people to choose their marriage partners, based on the view that love rather than parents' wishes is the most critical factor in selecting husbands or wives.

Another factor probably affecting intermarriage rates is a general weakening of the influence of religious communities in our society. Church-related considerations are weaker in affecting the actions of young people than they were several decades ago. Several researchers have charted changes in attitudes toward interfaith marriage. All found a trend toward greater acceptance.

Who Intermarries?

Much research has been done to discover which conditions motivate a young person to surmount the barriers of religious training, parental expectations, and social norms to enter into an inter-Christian marriage. One might expect that young persons whose parents are less committed to religious norms would be more likely to depart from their norms when choosing marriage partners. This is so; in every study, young persons from homes rated as not religiously devout or church-involved were found to be more willing to marry outside their faith. Even if the homes were religiously devout, family discord or parent-child tensions may weaken the effect of the parents, thus giving way to more inter-Christian or even inter-faith marriage. Intermarried persons, more so than intra-married persons, are likely to have felt dissatisfaction with parents and family relationships, to have had a strifeful family life, and to have been emancipated from their parents at the time of marriage. Also, children of mixed marriages are more likely to enter mixed marriages themselves.

The age of persons at marriage is another predictor of rates of intermarriage. Teenage marriages are especially likely to be religiously mixed, partly because teenage marriages often represent broken social norms. The youth culture's emphasis on romance and the purity of young love strengthens teenagers' attitudes that the views of adults in the community should be ignored. In short, if teenagers go ahead with early marriage against adults' wishes, they will similarly go ahead with intermarriage against adults' wishes. On the opposite side of the spectrum, older than average age at marriage is also associated with a higher rate of intermarriage, although to a lesser degree and for different reasons. Perhaps the limited supply of marriage partners for persons over age thirty makes for decreased concern about norms against religious intermarriage. Or possibly parental norms are almost nonexistent for persons in their late twenties or thirties. The incidence of intermarriage is also higher among those who have had more education than the average of their ethnic groups.

We might expect persons with solid religious orientation to have low intermarriage rates. In a cross-denominational study, this pattern was found in anti-ecumenical denominations such as the Mormons and the Seventh-day Adventists. However, in ecumenically minded denominations, the opposite pattern was obtained. There was more, not less, intermarriage among the more religiously committed. It has also been found that the strength of ethnic identification seems to inhibit intermarriage.

What Happens to the Religious Affiliation of the Intermarried?

When an Orthodox marries a non-Orthodox, the couple has five religious options:

1. The non-Orthodox can convert to the Orthodox Church.
2. The Orthodox can convert to the other Church.
3. Both can convert to a different but mutually acceptable Church.
4. Both can remain as they are.
5. Both can drop out of Church life entirely to escape the problem.

Which solution is the most common? Research provides some rough guesses. Some general sociological studies estimate that fifty percent of intermarriages involve a conversion in one direction, and the rest opt for either remaining as they are or both spouses can drop out of church life entirely to escape the problem. Is there a trend toward a higher or lower rate of unification of mixed marriages through conversion, either one way or the other? The young people feel less pressure today to unify a mixed marriage than they did a decade or two ago.

If one of the spouses converts, which one will it be? All research agrees that the relative devoutness of the two spouses is crucial – the less devout spouse usually converts to the Church of the more pious. Attitudes of families and in-laws are typically involved in the decision. There is also evidence that conversion tends toward the spouse with the higher social status. When conversions occur, research indicates that they usually appear near the time of the marriage or when the first child is less than ten years old. The marriage itself and the question of how to educate the first child produce the most conversions.

Finally, the religious involvement of intermarried couples who decide not to unify their marriage religiously is substantially lower than for other couples. A religiously mixed home tends to reduce the participation of the spouses in any Church. Church attendance by one spouse without the other is less meaningful, and the problems of children's education are always potential sources of tension.

Are Intermarriages Less Stable than Single-faith Marriages?

Research has looked at marital satisfaction of intermarriages and survival rates. Regarding marital satisfaction, several studies agree that mixed marriages are less satisfying than single-faith marriages. In a nationwide survey in the 1970s, respondents whose spouses were now of the same faith said they were pleased in their marriages to a greater extent than those who were religiously mixed. Several studies have looked at the problems of intermarriages. Couples who maintain their separate religions tend to have less marital happiness, partly because companionship is reduced, and in modern marriage, companionship is most valued. A significant problem is how to handle the religious training of children. Birth control, family size, and interference from in-laws regarding religious matters can also be troublesome.

Controversy abounds on the topic of survival rates, but the best studies show a higher survival rate for single-faith marriages than interfaith marriages. The most reliable conclusion is that interfaith marriages generally have lower marital satisfaction and lower survival rates, even if all other factors are controlled. One should remember that other factors and norms are potent in the making of a marriage.

Research on intermarriage demonstrates how much decisions are influenced by broad social forces. It also depicts the close relationships between family life and Church. Each supports the other, and when one weakens, the other suffers.

A Pastoral Approach

The traditional and still, to a large extent, negative approach of the Christian churches to intermarriages – an approach that emphasizes only differences, problems, and dangers – is no longer helpful when committed Christians of all confessions are intermarrying in such large numbers. The Orthodox Church has silently accepted inter-Christian marriage as a fact but does not explicitly advocate it. Pastoral prudence may keep us from encouraging intermarriages. Still, it is of the utmost importance that such marriage's unique character and potential be acknowledged. Currently, in pastoral practice, whenever there is an attempt to cope with intermarriages, the tension introduced by the divided religious loyalties of the spouses is attempted to be resolved unilaterally in favor of the Orthodox partner and the Orthodox Church. No value is ascribed to the faith commitment and Church membership of baptized Christian partners. Ironically, the situation in which the non-Orthodox party is lax or indifferent in religious matters is, for all practical purposes, favored, for this person is less likely to have sincere convictions that would pose obstacles to the Orthodox identity of the family; in fact, this kind of partner is viewed as a possible candidate for conversion. The notion of an inter-Christian marriage, in which the Christian of another confession has equal rights and is respected as a fellow believer, is only gradually impinging on the consciousness of the Churches.

The real problem that the Orthodox Church is facing today and chooses essentially to ignore is not that a spouse of one Christian confession marries a spouse of another but that there are different and competing Christian confessions. If a consumer mentality is applied to religious affiliations, people choose their Church according to the benefits/services that a particular Church may offer them. This means that members of small parishes with limited activities and programs who choose to intermarry tend to disidentify themselves from their community except if their parish has succeeded in instilling in them a strong identification with the community and pride in their identity. The same kind of disidentification impacts the members of "big" and "anonymous" parishes that have not developed a spirit of community and solidarity among their members.

The pastoral care of these families is not and cannot be the pastor's task alone but is the responsibility of the whole Church. Ecumenical families require exceptional pastoral sensitivity and patience from the entire community. It is straightforward for them to be alienated either by the pastor or the parishioners who do not adequately understand the dynamics of such families or are impatient with their commitments and affiliations to another Christian community or religion. One particular service that ecumenical couples, especially successful ecumenical couples, can and ought to offer to their parishes is the pastoral care of other ecumenical marriages. It is clear today that care is best delivered not by a pastor alone but in a peer-to-peer model by ecumenical couples who have gained valuable insights from their lived experience of ecumenical marriage.

Though pastoral care is the whole church's responsibility and never of pastors alone, pastors still have an essential responsibility. It is their task to preach the Gospel unceasingly to their congregations, to lead them to an ever more concrete understanding of the Gospel, and to empower them to enter into an ever-fuller practice of their servant mission. Pastors are to fulfill this task with all the means available to them – their preaching, their manifold teaching outside of liturgical gatherings, and the countless service groups organized in their parishes.

Since the time that an ecumenical couple needs to unify its religion spans from one to ten years – and sometimes even more – from their wedding, Orthodox pastors and faithful must accommodate and welcome "mixed" couples in their parishes. The non-Orthodox spouse should be encouraged to be involved in the community's life and assist in establishing connections with community members with similar educational backgrounds or social interests. If this kind of accommodation does not occur, then most likely, the couple will drop out of the parish. Orthodox faithful, because of their religious and ethnic composition, often resist such accommodations to non-Orthodox people since they consider them as a threat to their "changing" and "adopting" religious and ethnic identity. Yet, the future of our Church must make space for such "contextual" accommodations and simultaneously begin to think of ways to define and strengthen whatever is unique and irreplaceable in its ethos. From a theological perspective, it is essential to study the impact of ecumenical families in the life of our Church. What kind of future do we have as an ethnic and religious community because ethnicity is weakening and the number of ecumenical families is increasing? In other words, how do you reach people with various interests to whom essential Greek Orthodox identity could be more relevant? Is it possible for Orthodoxy to maintain its present canonical practices and uniqueness as a religious and ethnic community without a significant shrinkage in this country? Has a new Church just begun to emerge 'from below' as Orthodox members of ecumenical families through their non-Orthodox spouses or parents become members of another Church or religion?

I do not have an answer or answers to the questions that I have raised in this short paper. Still, I think the issue of mixed marriages has been proven to be complex without any practical solution that limits its impact on our community. One thing is for sure, and that is that becoming more "American," whether that means dropping the use of the Greek language and denouncing the ethnic element of our heritage, as some advocate, does not and will not solve the problem. Quite the contrary, the problem will become more severe since we will become captive of American religious minimalism that relativizes all doctrinal and historical differences between the churches to the extent that they worship God or believe in Jesus Christ and the Bible. On the other hand, the Greek Orthodox community's resistance to integrating linguistic and cultural elements into its immediate environment leads to an undesirable shrinkage of its size. Our Church's best option is to adopt flexible biculturalism and bilingualism, enriching its life by critically integrating the best elements of its Greek Orthodox faith and cultural heritage with the American culture. Suppose the Greek Orthodox community has the ambition to shape the ethos of its members. In that case, it needs to interpret social and personal realities to them by communicating its religious and cultural values and insights. I suspect that the Greek Orthodox community, together with many other religious and ethnic communities, is not very successful in communicating its value to its people whose mind is conditioned by many different cultural forces and consequently may not be receptive or concerned with its contribution to their lives. In response to this failure, Reform Jews, according to a story in *Newsweek* (July 22, 1991), have created a network of outreach programs that provides support and guidelines for both parents and children of inter-faith marriages. The point of these programs is to help adults become knowledgeable and committed Jews. According to the same story, this was an overdue step since most American Jews try to get through life with no more knowledge of Judaism than what a thirteen-year-old can master for his bar mitzvah. In today's America that apparently is not enough wisdom or commitment to maintain a durable identity as a Jew. Something similar has been done by other Christians in this continent whose problems are similar if not identical with ours. Since the challenge of mixed marriages is not a unique problem just for our Church, it is important to begin learning from others how we can cope with it without wasting precious energies and resources or even destroying precious elements of our heritage.

In conclusion, we need to think and develop strategies for sustaining the integrity of Greek Orthodox identity, values and institutions, including intra-group marriages. You cannot expect continuity if Greek Orthodox people know little about what they wish to continue. In that process we must build on whatever links, however weak, intermarried couples may still have with their heritage and welcome anyone who chooses to be identified as a Greek Orthodox.

XXVII

CHRIST AND THE POOR

While we celebrate the presence of our Lord Jesus Christ in the Divine Liturgy and in our parishes, there is a danger of neglecting His presence among the poor, the suffering, and the afflicted and paying lip service to the ethical teachings of our Church. By baptism, we participate in Christ's ministry for the world's salvation, which entails active concern for the poor and the afflicted. Every person of goodwill who follows Jesus in this world has the vocation to lessen the evil and suffering that prevails.

Jesus, in his teaching ministry, juxtaposed (Mt. 22.39 and Mk. 12.31) the demand of loving God with all one's heart (Deut. 6.5) with the command to love one's neighbor as oneself (Lev. 19.18). He urged his audience to understand each command by considering the other. St. Paul wrote to the Galatians: "Through love be servants of one another. For the whole law is fulfilled in one word, 'you shall love your neighbor as yourself'" (Gal. 5.13-14). The way that we love our neighbor reveals the authenticity of our faith in God in the most concrete terms (1 John 3.16-18).

Faith demands an active love toward people experiencing poverty and in need (James 2.15-17). St. Gregory of Nazianzus unequivocally stated that salvation depends on loving and showing compassion to the sick and poor: "We should fix in our minds the thought that the salvation of our bodies and souls depends on this: that we should love and show humanity to the suffering poor."

Charity and compassion are not virtues that only the wealthy must practice. It is the vocation that all people, even people with low incomes, should practice:

> Are you poor? There is someone much more flawed than you are. You have enough bread for ten days; another has enough for one. As a good and kindhearted person, distribute your surplus equally to needy people. Do not shrink from giving of the little you have; do not treat your calamity as if it is worse than the joint suffering... Believe in the one who always takes up the cause of the afflicted in his person and supplies grace from his store.

The pastoral nature of the Church's faith did not allow the issue of poverty in situations of famine, homelessness, and sickness to be simply an issue of theological speculation. The Church encouraged the faithful to be compassionate and use their resources to manifest their faith in God. St. Gregory of Nazianzus implored his audience: "Let nothing come between your will and the deed. This alone must suffer, not delay kindness to another person ... a kindness done promptly is a kindness twice done. A favor done in a sour spirit, and because you must, is unlovely and without grace. We should be cheerful, not grieving when we give mercy."

Identification of Christ with the Poor

Based on Matthew 25.31-46, Christians believe Christ is mysteriously present in the poor and the needy. St. Gregory of Nyssa reminds the rich that we must recognize the identity of the poor with Christ and acknowledge their unique dignity and place in the Christian community.

> Do not despise these men in their abjection; do not think them of no account. Reflect on what they are, and you will understand their dignity; they have taken the person of our Savior upon them. For he, the compassionate, has lent them his person to bash the unmerciful and the haters of the poor... The poor are the treasures of the good things that we look for, the keepers of the gates of the Kingdom, opening them to the merciful.

For St. John Chrysostom, the poor become the liturgical images of the holiest elements in all Christian worship: the altar and the body of Christ. He explicitly identifies the poor as a divine and divinely constituted altar.

> Do you wish to see his altar?… This altar is composed of the very members of Christ, and the body of the Lord becomes your altar… venerable because it is Christ's body…This altar you can see lying everywhere, in the alleys and the agoras, and you can sacrifice upon it anytime… invoke the spirit not with words but with deeds.

Based on this sacramental identification of Christ with the poor, he suggests specific ways to express the recognition that Christ lives and is actively present in the poor and needy people:

> Do you wish to pay homage to Christ's body? Then do not neglect him when he is naked. At the same time that you honor him here [in Church] with hangings made of silk, do not ignore him outside when he perishes from cold and nakedness. The One who said, "This is my body,"…also said, "When I was hungry, you gave me nothing to eat. "

XXVIII

POLITICS AND CHRISTIAN FAITH

Americans are deeply divided and polarized in their political stances and choices. The divisiveness and polarization in the American political realm have also affected Christian communities even though some of them have chosen to ignore the challenges that politics raise to the Church's witness's integrity to the world.

The relation of politics and Christian faith is a highly complex issue that deserves careful attention since Christian faith and politics determine, to a great extent, people's personal and collective life. As we address religion's relation with politics, it is imperative to be cautious not to reduce or surrender the one to the other, or vice-versa. Furthermore, because of the complex nature of the relationship between religion and politics, we must resist the temptation to consider our thoughts on this matter as a final prescription of how Christian Churches should identify the root causes of the political challenges and choose the issues that deserve their thoughtful contribution.

Sacred and Secular: A False Dichotomy

In Christian circles, the Church's witness to the world is often contrasted with her sacred otherworldly tradition. Through political actions and involvement, it is often suggested that the Church skirts from her primary sacred responsibility. She substitutes immanence for transcendence. She replaces the Gospel of love and forgiveness with social reforms, legislative change, political programs, and actions. Thus, by focusing so much on social and political matters, the Churches increasingly fail in their sacred mission, to unite the world with God. They become inauthentic.

If such an attitude prevails, the Churches consciously choose to ignore the political challenges. The vision of the Church is ruptured into sacred and profane since evangelization and civilization, transcendence and immanence, Gospel and culture, religion, and politics are conceived as distinct and separate and often incompatible entities.

This posture minimizes how God's grace operates beyond the visible boundaries of the institutional Church and undermines the public witness of the Church in a plural and democratic society. Thus, it individualizes the Gospel, the coming reality of God's reign, which affects all human aspects of life. For these reasons, an increasing number of theologians believe that politics as an embodiment of the values and principles that govern the people's collective life cannot be ignored. Politics, whether we like it or not, affect the mode and quality of people's lives. As a result, neutrality on political matters cannot be a viable option for Christians who have a specific theological vision of how the world should be and how people should relate to one another. There is an intimate connection without confusion between Christian faith and politics. While evangelization is the Church's essential mission, the distinctive vocation of the Church, actions for justice that promote a culture of peace are constitutive dimensions of the Churches' mission.

Why do Christians not agree among themselves about the political implications of the faith? The polarization of the political interpretation of the Gospel leads us to question whether Christian faith is the premise upon which Christians build their political identity in the world or is their identity shaped by their narrowly defined self-interest, fears, and insecurities? Are Christians prisoners of the world, or does their faith transform their vision of the world and inform their political options? There is a danger, already evident in American society, that religious people in their political choices are overconfident and dismissive of the others' since they believe that their political decisions reflect not merely their opinions but also of God's will. Such a posture may become the basis of violently dismissing of the others' who adhere to different worldviews. In general, people never understand enough about the social situation or the political implications of their choices. When devout people become politically engaged, there is a temptation to advocate ultimate solutions and radical actions to socioeconomic and political challenges. In such a posture, Christians forget the basic theological fact that leading solutions to social problems must be linked to the "eschaton" that comes by God's initiative as a gift to His people and not only as a human accomplishment.

The Task of the Christian Church in Politics

The essential task of the Church's involvement in politics is to demythologize the prevailing false absolutization of the power of politics to change the world, although it may, in some instances, improve the life of the world at least in some instances. Religion should help politics to be both thoughtful and less self-confident. Whatever politics understand as a human reality should complement the transcendent salvific dimension of God's presence in history that the Church witnesses through her life and mission. If this is not done, the Church loses herself by becoming just another political and human organization.

The Church proclaims to the world the coming of God's reign, which signifies the world's ultimate humanization. From this perspective, all political ideologies and actions as human products are provisional. They contain in themselves essential imperfections, which give rise to social alienation and suffering despite their professed benevolent intention. The Church should unveil the despair and the separation that human political ideologies have caused to the world. Simultaneously, she urges the world to move beyond them by offering herself a model of how the world should be in its true nature. But, before she becomes an agency of social criticism within the realm of politics, she must reveal God's new creation in her life. Thus, in exercising her critical functions within the political domain, the Church becomes a humanizing force of progress that pulls the world towards a better future.

The Church in faithfulness to Gospel cannot remain silent in the face of gross injustice and violence. If the Church does not become the voice of the voiceless, she betrays her prophetic task and dangerously assaults her credibility. However, this is far from suggesting that the Church should propose specific social, economic, and political programs beyond her nature and competence.

Church leaders must not seek to identify themselves with political leaders as a sign of their authority in the world. They should avoid a narrow partisan position on political issues. Their role is not to leap into the political arena themselves but to make the people sensitive to what enhances and diminishes human life. The practical policies designed to achieve such ends should be the work of laypeople. The Church needs to realize that the ministry of the laity is not just an amateurish and pale imitation of the ministry of the ordained The Church should be involved in politics mostly through the laity who, hopefully, struggle to translate their Christian faith into concrete actions. In this process, a mutually enriching dialogue between politicians and faithful Christians is desirable. This dialogue may take a variety of forms. In some instances, the Church may also opt to take radical prophetic actions against evil, violence, injustice, and human suffering that politics may institutionalize through its executive power.

The Church becomes a credible witness of the Gospel as she is constantly becoming, through God's Spirit, a community of persons who relate with each other in love, peace, and justice in the image of the three persons' relations of the Trinity. It is the existence of such a community that enables the world to move closer and closer to its true nature. The credibility of the Church's message in the political arena depends not on what she proclaims to be but on what she does.

XXIX

VIOLENCE AND RELIGION

Conflicts among persons, communities, and nation-states that lead to violence seem to surge upwards despite the promise of modernity that violent clashes will be gradually obliterated as societies and people become more reasonable and enlightened. Those who commit acts of violence claim that their actions advance the course of peace and proper order as they perceive that good order. Such people or communities become more ruthless against their opponents if they view their participation in violent acts not only as a tribute to peace aimed at restoring proper social order but as a religious duty.

Violence is a paradoxical beast. Its civilizing name is coercion. In the dictionary, the word violence is defined as the exertion of physical force to injure or abuse; an instance of violent treatment or procedure; injury by or as if by distortion, infringement, or profanation; an intense, turbulent, or furious and often destructive action or force. From a theological perspective, it is possible to agree that violence is an element of this world, and it does not have any relationship with the coming reign of God or the life of Jesus. They reveal the power of God in the kenotic love of the Cross.

Society uses violence to legitimize its social agencies and give order to its life by distributing power and resources. This ordering function of society never leads to one single, finite order and cannot help generating disorder alongside order, injustice alongside justice, and ambivalence alongside clarity. As a result, coercion is always an ambivalent force of societal integration and disintegration. It never succeeds in establishing the perfect societal order and distribution of power and resources. Thus, the process of ordering life in society and re-distributing energy and resources will never have an end in this world.

In the modern world, the State monopolizes the legitimate use of force within a given territory. The State enforces law and order, and its use of coercion is widely accepted. Others who try to establish their own subjective, self-serving, and arbitrary order use force illegitimately. Coercion as an ambivalent social reality is recognized as necessary and gratuitous, desirable and undesirable, beneficial and harmful. In its civilizing version, it is called "enforcement of law and order" that the State exercises, while the rest of the coercion in any given society is called violence. What this distinction hides, though, is that whatever we describe with the nasty word violence is also about specific ordering and specific laws to be enforced – only those are not the order and regulations that the maker of this distinction had in mind. This distinction stands for the designed order and all the rest: between the controlled and uncontrolled, the regular and erratic, the predictable and unpredictable, the foreseeable and the unexpected, the grounded and the contingent, and the reasonable and the senseless. Zygmunt Bauman[1] rightly observes that order-keeping and violence are endemically contested. It is never conclusively drawn: the borderline barriers stay effective only as long as there are heavily armed men to guard them. The difference between controlled and uncontrolled space is between civility and barbarity. The same social critic writes: "In the land of civility, no coercion (ideally) comes by surprise and from unexpected quarters; it can be rationally calculated, become the 'known necessity' one can even celebrate as freedom. In the land of barbarity, coercion (here called violence) is diffused, dispersed, erratic – and thus unpredictable and incapacitating."[2]

Violence as an unpredictable and arbitrary use of power in its

---

1 Zygmunt Bauman, Life in Fragments: Essays in Postmodern Morality (Cambridge: Blackwell, 1995), p. 141.
2 Ibid.p.143.

destructive expressions is a senseless and cruel human act. People commit cruelties against each other after they have developed justifications for their neighbor's pain. Such justifications provide them with moral insensitivity. They do not feel any responsibility for the other's life and suffering. People massively participate in cruel deeds as they disassociate moral guilt from their acts. According to Bauman, this is achieved through *adiaphorization*, which makes specific actions morally neutral. The modern organization achieves just that with its scientific management and coordination of human actions. It enthrones procedural discipline and personal loyalty as the all-overriding criterion of moral performance. It further hides the link between partial actions and the ultimate effects of coordinated moves. Modern technology has increased the power of *adiaphorization* by the massive volume of exposure to images of human suffering that leads its spectators to moral insensitivity. It is also accurate that electronic weapons of mass destruction have created a distance between the perpetrators of cruelty and their victims since human bodies are seen in electronic identification tools as targets, not as discernible human bodies. Innocent victims of such weapons do not evoke any sense of guilt in anyone since they are considered to be "computer or logistical mistakes."

The fragmentation of the process into a series of self-contained and self-enclosed episodes without past consequences does not allow the construction of lasting networks of mutual duties and obligations. Marriages, families, parenthood, neighborhoods, and workplaces have lost much of their function of managing factory order. Even the state has begun surrendering to deregulated and privatized market forces in its societal integrative and ordering functions. Thus, the field is open to imagine and postulate communities to supply collective identities recognized as necessary entry points for individuals to societal life. This gives rise to neo-tribalism. "Neo-tribalism is bad news for all wishing to see discourse and argument replacing knives and bombs as tools of self-assertion."

Although religious communities proclaim peace and express their resolve to work for its realization, they contribute to conflicts and intolerance. Social scientists believe that religious communities, because of the particularity of their universal message, will continue to be simultaneously, for some, a force of universality and peace. In contrast, it will be a source of division, exclusion, and conflict for others. As different communities of people achieve a relative just or an adequate distribution of power, a favorable recognition of their presence and interests in modern society, and become painfully aware of violence's dehumanizing effects upon its victims, a search for peace begins. In such a context, religious communities will turn to their history and classic texts, trying to retrieve the peace-loving aspects of their tradition.

The involvement of Churches in moments of peace, healing, and reconciliation is primarily therapeutic and not preventive. The memory, however, of their involvement and complicity in acts of violence cannot be easily forgotten by those who expected the Churches to be the presence of God's reconciling and healing grace in the world. The Churches' prophetic witness in conflict situations depends on their particular ways of understanding the nature of their witness in the world. It can be seriously limited by ill-conceived actions that intend to communicate God's healing grace. Instead, they reflect people's subjective ideology, which fortifies their particular interests and leads them to greater acts of violence. Sometimes, the Churches, for various reasons, may opt to speak against violence and injustice in such general and abstract terms that their voice does not have any transformative impact on the life of the world and even the life of their parishioners. This is especially true in the modern differentiated society in which people may profess love for God, peace, justice, and reconciliation in the religious aspect of their personal lives, but as they enter into other social subsystems, become aggressive, uncompromising, unjust, and vengeful according to the functional rationality that prevails in them.

XXX

PEACE, ECONOMIC INJUSTICE, AND THE ORTHODOX CHURCH

The peacemaking vocation of the Church is a dynamic process of a never-ending personal and communal transformation that reflects the human and fallible struggle to participate in God's Trinitarian life. St. Nicholas Cabasilas epigrammatically summarizes the Orthodox view on peacemaking: "Christians, as disciples of Christ, who made all things for peace, are to be 'craftsmen of peace.' They are a peaceable race since nothing is more characteristic of a Christian than to be a worker for peace." Effective intervention in situations of conflict and oppression requires the Churches not to ignore what is possible to learn from advances in political sciences and economics and from successful economic and political policies and practices that aim to transform conflicts into life opportunities.

In addressing the root causes of injustice and violence in the marketplace, the Orthodox Church recognizes the autonomy of the inherent rationality of the market and leaves the development of economic theories and policies to those who understand its dynamics better. The Church, however, critiques economic ideas and practices based on their performance and their effects on people. Her criticism contributes toward a revisionary market logic that favors financial methods that generate more significant opportunities for a more equitable and just distribution of power and resources.

One-and-a-half billion people live in areas affected by instability, conflict, or large-scale, organized criminal violence. The causes of conflict arise from economic, political, and security dynamics. Political exclusion and inequality affecting regional, religious, or ethnic groups are associated with higher risks of civil war. In comparison, inequality between richer and poorer households relates to increased threats of violence. The disparity between the rich and poor between and within nations is rising. Unemployment is rising, pushing more people into poverty, malnutrition, poor health, depression, violence, insecurity, fear, and desperation. There are nearly one billion undernourished people on our planet, and this number is increasing by sixty-eight people every minute; more than one every second. The human cost of violence cannot be ignored by anyone who considers all human beings to be icons of God.

The Orthodox Church understands the economic and monetary crisis that leads to an increased disparity between rich and poor, primarily as a spiritual and cultural crisis. Its causes are unrestrained individualism that leads to an excessive desire for wealth and consumerism. Individualism and consumerism have disconnected people from God's love and their neighbor, thus preventing them from reflecting in their lives on God's love for all creation.

St. John Chrysostom stated that not being an advocate of the poor would be "the worst inhumanity." Being the advocate of the poor led him to refute all the arguments by which the affluent justified the marginalization of the poor and their indifference towards them. Christ, in an intimate manner, is identified with the poor. The poor are not the spectacle of human misery and suffering that evokes compassion or disgust, but they are the icons of Christ, the presence of Christ in the broken world. If you refuse to give bread to the poor, you ignore Christ who desires to be fed: "You eat in excess; Christ eats not even what he needs... At the moment, you have taken possession of the resources that belong to Christ, and you consume them aimlessly."[1] The poor for St. John Chrysostom is the liturgical

---

1 On Matthew, Homily 48.8

image of the holiest elements in all Christian worship: the altar and the body of Christ. He states:

> Do you wish to see his altar?...This altar is composed on the very members of Christ, and the body of the Lord becomes your altar... venerable because it is itself Christ's body... This altar you can see lying everywhere, in the alleys and in the agoras and you can sacrifice upon it anytime... invoke the spirit not with words but with deeds.[2]

The Orthodox Church advocates a culture of compassion in which people share their material resources with those in need. Charity and compassion are not virtues practiced just by those with the material resources and means. Instead, they are virtues that promote Christians' communal love for all human beings. Whether rich or poor, every human being must be charitable and compassionate to those lacking the essential material resources for sustenance. St. Basil the Great encourages the poor to share even the minimal goods they may have. Almsgiving leads people to God and grants all the resources needed to sustain and develop their human potential. However, a voluntary sharing of resources in the present world is not enough. Building a culture of peace demands global and local institutional changes and new economic practices that address at a more fundamental level the root causes of poverty. It calls for a fusion of the Christian culture of compassion with the knowledge we have acquired through experience and social science advances about the structural sources of poverty and its multifaceted aspects that urgently need to be addressed through concerted reflective actions.

In an increasingly fragmented world, the Orthodox Church acknowledges and defends the dignity of every human being and cultivates human solidarity. In addressing violence in the marketplace, even if people accept the virtues of justice and peace in their hearts, the market operates with its autonomous logic and economic practices. It is guided by the belief that there can

---

2 *Epistulam 2 ad Corinthios*, Homilia 50.4.

be a total free market in which unregulated competing financial relationships of individuals in pursuit of their economic gains can lead to optimum good. It advocates those free markets without government interference would be the most efficient and socially optimal allocation of resources. Many economists and institutions of global development agencies embrace economic globalization as an indisputable reality and suggest that there is no alternative to this. They assume that neoliberalism contributes to all nations' prosperity and equitable development. Unfortunately, though, its economic practices have not been designed to meet the immediate needs of the world's poor people. As a result, global inequalities between nations and within nations are widening. Joseph Stiglitz, former World Bank Chief Economist (1997-2000) and Nobel laureate in economics, notes that economic globalization in its current form risks exacerbating poverty and increasing violence if not checked because it is impossible to separate economic issues from social and political issues.

The Orthodox Church is not in a position to suggest concrete alternatives to economic globalization. The Church neither intends to endorse or reject complex economic policies and practices that regulate the global economy. Yet, based on the eschatological orientation of the Christian gospel, Orthodoxy believes that all political and economic theories and methods are subject to criticism and modification to overcome those aspects that generate violence and injustice. The logic of the market must not only seek the maximization of profits favoring and serving only those with economic capital and power. Financial practices must ensure just and sustainable development for all people. We cannot talk about a free economy without judging what kinds of exchange are conducive to the flourishing of life and what kinds are not. The Churches are led by their faith to actively foster economic practices that reflect God's peace and justice. In their logic, these financial practices integrate those elements of social life that promote a culture of compassion that unites all human beings in peace and justice. Indispensable aspects of this culture respect all human beings' dignity and rights, equitable socio-economic relationships, broad participation in economic and political decision-making, and just sharing of resources and power.

Once we put human faces to millions of people who suffer the consequences of inequitable distribution of power and resources, it becomes evident that the Church's mission to the world entails involvement in noble efforts to eradicate poverty and injustice through prayer expressed in thoughtful actions.

XXXI

THE CRISIS OF
RACIAL INJUSTICE AND INEQUITY

On June 4, 2020, the leadership of four interfaith organizations – Religions for Peace USA, Parliament of World Religions (PoWR), United Religions Initiative (URI), and the Interfaith Center of New York (ICNY) – issued a statement: "This Perilous Moment: A Statement from Religious Leaders and Communities on the Crisis of Racial Injustice and Inequity and Current Protests."[1] This statement is important, as Jews, Christians, Muslims, Buddhists, Hindus, Baha'i, Humanists, Indigenous, Jains, Sikhs, Taoists, Unitarian Universalists, Zoroastrians, and many others signed on to the statement and were able to address the systemic evil of racism that plagues our country in one voice and with a sense of urgency. Drawing inspiration and empowerment from the spiritual resources of their respective tradition, each faith community is underscoring their commitment to justice, peace, and reconciliation.

The Orthodox Church, through its participation in Religions for Peace USA, actively jointly works for the promotion of peace and coexistence with other faith communities. Her participation in these

---

1 "This Perilous Moment: A Statement from Religious Leaders and Communities on the Crisis of Racial Injustice and Inequity and Current Protests," https://www.rfp.org/resources/religions-for-peace-condemns-mob-attack-on-us-capitol/ last accessed July 8, 2025

efforts reflects her ethos, as it has been authoritatively expressed in the Great and Holy Council (Crete 2016) to seek inter-religious understanding and cooperation to advance peaceful coexistence and harmonious living. His All-Holiness Ecumenical Patriarch Bartholomew, in his address to the Global Peace Conference of Al-Azhar and Muslim Council of Elders (2017), expressed the belief of the Orthodox Church in the need for human solidarity and the commitment of the Orthodox Church to advancing that goal through interfaith collaboration building a culture of justice and peace. He stated that the credibility of religious communities today depends on whether they are active advocates and guardians of the human dignity and freedom of all people. His All-Holiness has suggested that it is only through dialogue and collaboration that faith-based communities, governments, and civil society can respond together to the challenge of building a just and peaceful world.
He stated:

> We can face these challenges only together. Nobody – not a nation, state, religion, science, and technology – can face the current problems alone. We need one another; we need common mobilization, efforts, goals, and spirit. Therefore, we regard the present multifaceted crisis as an opportunity for practicing solidarity, dialogue and cooperation, openness and confidence. Our future is common, and the way toward this future is a common journey. As it is written in the Psalms: "Behold now, what is so good or so pleasant as for brothers to dwell together in unity?" (Psalm 133.1)

Advancing the cause of justice, peace, and reconciliation is primarily an act of God. The faithful, filled with God's love for all humanity, are co-creators with God, creating a world that reflects God's love, peace, and justice as much as possible. Liberation from injustice, oppression, racism, and violence in today's world requires the collaboration of the Church with other faith communities and people of God based on their shared humanity and their God-given vocation to love one another. The joint statement issued by four interfaith organizations described today as a "perilous moment" and underscored the shared necessity to work together to combat the injustice, oppression, racism, and violence in American society. This statement is not an abstract discussion about an otherworldly realm of existence – it reflects the conflictual nature of history. It recognizes the evil of racism, white supremacy, and police brutality against African Americans that has justifiably contributed to an explosion of justified and righteous anger.

In the statement, the faith communities jointly recognized that the "wicked scourge of discrimination and racism is structural, systemic, systematic, and institutional." The origins of this systemic evil that plagues the country are cultural, economic, political, and social factors, as well as spiritual and moral factors. The legacy of racism affects every aspect – "seen and unseen" – of our personal and communal life. The religious communities jointly admit that they are complicit in the evil of racism and injustice because of their long silence and lack of action. They recognize that, in many ways, false tenets of their respective religious tradition have been used to perpetuate the evil of racism. "Our sacred texts and traditions have been used, wrongly so, to further racial injustice." However, religious traditions are, in their view, "a deep well" from which they draw inspiration and power that empower them to be agents of peace and justice. "People of faith must stand for love and equity, equality, and justice." Religious communities, including the Orthodox Church, once they acknowledge that their faith has been manipulated for oppressive and unjust purposes, must identify those aspects of their tradition that promote justice, human dignity, and the rights of all people. They should review their religious education programs and their spiritual traditions, trying to identify better ways to raise the consciousness of the faithful concerning their responsibility to respect and care for all people who are beloved children to God regardless of their world views, race, color, or culture. Interfaith collaboration and dialogue provide opportunities for all committed and involved religious communities to critically rediscover aspects of their respective tradition as they seek to address issues of common concern. Yet, it is essential to recognize that within each of the faith communities, there will be people who, for a variety of reasons, have embraced in faith a "tribal God" and refuse to recognize the universality of God's love that demands from them to love, care, and respect humanity in its diverse racial, religious, cultural, and ethnic existence.

The evolving social unrest and the polarization that the evil of racism has ignited challenges religious communities, civil society, and governments to hear the voices of the suffering people and address their legitimate concerns. In trying to quell social unrest, the statement of the religious communities rightly warns that each of the actions that people take "represents steps towards one of two possible different paths: inclusive democracy or authoritarian state." The interfaith community has unreservedly opted to "decisively walk towards an inclusive democracy, where faiths and freedoms flourish." They must responsibly "act now" and live with intention through the discomfort of this crisis and all the things that require faith communities to co-steward the healing society needs. Of course, such an active involvement in the process of social transformation and reconciliation that aims to eradicate the evil of injustice and discrimination should be grounded not in a particular political ideology but in the "deep wellsprings" of each religious community's faith in fostering hope, justice, and reconciliation. The practical expression of their respective faith traditions to the current situation requires people of faith to educate themselves about the genuine impacts of racism and sojourn with movements led by persons of color for justice, equality, and equity. A dynamic witness of the religious communities against the evil of racism in all of its insidious forms includes participating in protests, calling out racial injustices, and partnering with affected communities. Religious communities must also encourage volunteerism and philanthropic commitments to institutions advancing racial justice and harmony.

Thus, the faith communities do not remain indifferent, praying to God to bring healing and reconciliation. Still, they dare to take sides: "We are here to stand with those who are rightly and justifiably enraged at police brutality and racial injustice and who feel unheard and unheeded in their lamentations." They join their voices and actions with the protestors as they pray unceasingly for peace and justice to prevail and for the healing of the hearts of all those feeling the pain of these traumas. This, however, does not mean that they condone irrational explosions of violence and looting. Looting is viewed as a distraction from the main reasons their collective concerns gave rise to protest demonstrations in the beginning – namely, addressing racial injustice, police brutality, and white supremacy.

Police brutality, as a tragic epiphenomenon of systemic racism that needs to be addressed, should not become a pretext for dismissing the importance of law enforcement for people's safety and well-being. "Law enforcement has an important and vital role in our society to serve and protect all of us, and we support their peaceable actions to uphold just laws." People must trust that the rule of law is applied fairly and equitably to all parties. Political leaders, as well as law enforcement, must ensure that people have the space and freedom to express their will through constructive, peaceful protests against all forms of injustice and racism.

The systemic nature of racism, violence, and injustice requires "a longform response effort that will span generations." Even if the moral anger subsides and the attention of the mass media has shifted to other matters (though they should not), faith communities must continue to pray with their "feet and hands" and work together to resolve the insidious impacts of the ugly legacy of slavery, the blight of racism, and the multiple forms of discrimination in our communities. The religious communities would give credence to their joint vision of an inclusive society by advocating changes, not only in the society but also in their internal life, by supporting efforts at diversity, equity, and inclusion in their places of worship, workplaces, and lives.

XXXII

HUMAN DIGNITY

Human dignity is foundational in the imagination of many desperate people worldwide who dream of greater justice and freedom in their personal and communal spaces. Respect for human dignity and recognition of human rights demand the development of a culture of peace and justice.

Orthodox theologians have increasingly begun to debate the issue of human dignity and rights. The Orthodox critique of the human rights tradition focuses on its reduction, especially in affluent Western countries, to a basis that fortifies the self, leads to self-centeredness, and legitimizes self-gratification. This undoubtedly contributes to social fragmentation that endangers human solidarity, love, and communion – necessary elements and norms for a compassionate and just community. While the criticism of Orthodoxy against the philosophical and theological basis of the human rights tradition may be an essential remedy to its current crisis, Orthodox theologians must also be critical of oppressive communal structures of dominance that do not allow people to be different or do not recognize their differences within their communal life. In other words, the turn to subjectivity developed in the West may be an essential corrective to the totalistic inclinations of communal life. At the same time, the Orthodox emphasis on communal life and the importance of relations is an equally important corrective to Western individualism and social fragmentation. Our choice is not either/or. Neither is it an issue of balance between human subjectivity and community but a continuous reflexive relationship of mutual enrichment.

Orthodox Churches living in oppressive contexts as persecuted and oppressed minorities appeal to the notion of human dignity and rights for their survival and participation in communal life with dignity and freedom. The recognition that the idea of human dignity and rights has captured the imagination of people throughout the world who desire to live free from oppressive external powers, along with the current global discussions about human dignity and rights, is an invitation for Orthodox theology to contribute, in an intelligible and communicable language, its spiritual resources and insights. The conversation of Orthodoxy with other Christian traditions and religious and secular ideologies on human dignity may bring freshness and clarity to theological anthropology, which has not been one of the liveliest areas of theology.

For Christian thought, human dignity is grounded on the biblical and patristic tradition that humans are created in God's image. Human existence has its origins, sustenance, and maturation in loving relationships with God, significant others, and the material world. These relationships are not external, attached to an existing human substance; they are internal and constitutive of human identity. Human beings exist within a set of structures of relationships, which are constitutive of their being. The crucial question is how we actively contribute to the relationships that shape our identity. Do we, for instance, recognize the created sociality of all human beings, or do we contradict it by constructing our subjectivity as a denial of all sociality? Furthermore, given that relationships can be either life-enhancing or dehumanizing, it is important to seek, develop, and sustain relationships that allow and promote the flourishing of life for all human beings.

Christian theological anthropology locates the human primarily not in the relationship of humans to themselves (i.e., capacity for reflection, self-consciousness) or their relationship to the world but in God, whose love as life-giving reality is extended unconditionally to all. Human dignity is a quality humans possess, independent of their capacity in their relationship to themselves or the world.

The satisfaction of each human being originates in God's creating, redeeming, and deifying grace that enables human beings to transcend their self-existence and move towards the fullness of their humanity in life-sustaining and life-transforming relations. Only in communion do human beings become genuinely what they are destined to be by God.

Though theology and secular thinking have a sense of human dignity as universal, they handle this in very different ways. Human dignity in theology is primarily seen as God's unconditional gift to everyone. In contrast, for others, it is viewed as an inherent quality of each human being as an essential self. There are, however, different ways in which something can be experienced as a gift. It is possible for people to feel demeaned or patronized by being told that something is a gift when they think it is an essential part of their nature or constitution or something to which they are entitled. For others, however, receiving a gift is a highly affirming experience and something to be welcomed. Seeing dignity as a gift carries tasks and obligations appropriate to good stewardship of the facility, whereas seeing it as a right carries no such responsibility. When a Christian tradition speaks of something being a gift of God, though the latter is intended, sometimes, in the context of post-enlightenment thought, it is heard as being patronizing.

In Christian theology, everything that is appropriate for human beings is the gift of God. Thus, human dignity is not a self-grounded possession enjoyed apart from a relationship with the Creator, Redeemer, and Sanctifier. As Chrysostom writes memorably in a sermon on Philippians, "Humans possess the dignity of rational nature, but this comes to them as a gift, not as something they have earned. Hence, there is no natural preeminence amongst us, for no good thing is naturally our own."[1] Because God confers human dignity, its measure and norm are to be discovered not in social conventions but in God and the pattern of God's action toward humankind in creation and redemption in Christ. In response to critics of Christianity who found it ridiculous that "poor, unskilled

---

1 Homilies on Philippians 7, *NPNF*, series 1, vol. 13, p. 213

people should dispute about heavenly things," Minucius Felix (late second or third century) replied, "Let him know that all men are begotten alike, with a capacity and ability of reasoning and feeling, without preference of age, sex, or honor."[2]

The perception that every human has inherent dignity insufficient to embrace the totality of life, theologically, is seen as a static notion. It leaves no scope for a dynamic unfolding of God's purpose for human dignity. A Christian theology of dignity needs to be balanced by an eschatological approach; creation is a continuing process and, consequently, inseparable from eschatology. This requires that we distinguish different senses of dignity. In one sense, we already have dignity, but in another, we do not have dignity in all its fullness. There is both a present actuality and a future potentiality about human dignity. Both are essential to an adequate theology of dignity. Holding the doctrine of creation and eschatology together shows us how the whole or universal concept of human dignity must always be about a relative or qualitative one.

A theology of creation gives us an absolute concept of dignity that bestows dignity on all without variations or exceptions. However, this affirmation needs to be complemented by a qualitative idea of dignity that reflects the extent to which the potential that comes from being made in the image of God is or has been realized. The distinction between being made in the image of God and growing in his likeness has been used in this way. People differ to the extent they have realized the potential that comes from being created in the image of God. At present, the fuller dignity to which we all are called and for which we can hope is more wholly realized in some people than others. However, all are called to fully realize the dignity that is part of God's purpose. People can thus live in the space created between the basic dignity given to them and the fuller dignity to which they are called. It makes a crucial difference in how this is experienced. The good human experience of dignity depends on keeping open the axis between the dignity we already

---

2 *ANF*, vol. 4, p. 181.

have as a gift and the fuller dignity we are promised and toward which we are called. To see dignity solely as a necessary property of human beings, as Enlightenment thought tends to do, is to lose touch with the eschatological promise that the dignity of humanity can become more of a reality.

On the other hand, if dignity is seen entirely as something that might develop more fully in the future, with no sense that it is already in some fundamental sense present, there would be no constraints on everyday indignities. Suppose the only concept of dignity we can affirm in the political realm of life is the universal dignity of all as an inherent quality of every human being. In that case, it might be assumed that human dignity could be neither destroyed nor improved upon. Only if there is a sense that human dignity could become more of a reality than is presently the case can people be motivated to improve human conditions. This sense of dignity as something that remains to be realized can be seen as an invitation and promise, a possibility that is held out to people and to which they are invited to respond.